GREAT DAY OUT?

WHERE CAN YOU GET A PARENT & TODDLER PASS?

WHERE CAN YOU GET THE WORLD'S FIRST PITCH BLACK BACKWARDS PLUMMETING RIDE?

Welcome to the 10th edition for Beds, Bucks & Herts.
Researched by Karen Gilmore.

CONTENTS

HOW TO USE THE GUIDE

 MAP REFERENCES - Locate the grid squares on the Map on page 4. Attractions are listed in alphabetical order within each grid square. At a glance you can see what else is in the grid square. You will need a more detailed map to navigate with.

Ⓐ PRICE CODE (defined in key on most pages) to help you budget your visits.

Schools SCHOOL PARTY FACILITIES - Ideal for all school visit planning.

🎈 BIRTHDAY PARTIES ORGANISED - This could solve the problem of looking for a new idea to make it the best Birthday Party ever!

Open all year WINTER OPENING - See at a glance where you can go in the Winter.

ACCURACY

This publication is designed to provide accurate information but such information may be changed without notice by the bodies concerned and information herein should therefore be only used as a guide.

Cube Publications, Bank House, Mavins Road, Farnham, Surrey GU9 8JS
Phone/Fax 01252 722761 or 01425 615648
Published by Cube Publications. Printed by Southbourne Printing Co. Ltd. Artwork by Ted Evans Design. Photography by Sue Bennett.

ISBN 1 871808 63 4

MAP

Scale

0 — miles — 10

KEY

- - - County Boundary
——— Major Road
━━━ Motorway

★ LET'S GO Guide available now

1

Stoke Bruerne •

NORTHANTS
★

Bromham •

Olney •

Bedford

★ CAMBS

BEDS

A6

Sandy •

Biggleswade

Clophill •

Ampthill •

2

Milton Keynes

• Buckingham   Bletchley •

Woburn •

A5

A1(M)

Royston •   Bishops Stortford

Letchworth •

BUCKS

Leighton Buzzard •

Hitchin •

A10

M1

ESSEX

3

• Quainton

A41

Dunstable •

Luton   • **Stevenage**

• Knebworth

Aylesbury

Waddesdon •

Welwyn Garden City •

Tring •

HERTS

Ware •

Haddenham •

Berkhamsted •

Hatfield •

Hertford

Princes Risborough •

A413

St Albans

Hoddesdon •

Chesham •
Amersham •

Hemel Hempstead •

OXON ★

High Wycombe

Watford

M25

Marlow •   Beaconsfield •

M40

4

★ SURREY

BERKSHIRE
★

A   B   C

4

FUN FOR FREE

This chapter includes museums, a selection of parks, open spaces and other places that freely offer family entertainment and enjoyment. Although free admission, there may be some car parking charges, extra charges for schools and special activities, or requests for donations.

MAP REFS

A1-B4

Waymarked Routes. The Upper and Lower Icknield Way, the North Buckinghamshire Way and the Ridgeway itself which starts at Ivinghoe Beacon, cut through parts of Buckinghamshire offering wonderful waymarked walks.

A2 *Open all year* — **Bourton Park,** Old Bourton Road, **Buckingham** is a large, informal park with a river running through it. There are hard surfaced paths, bridges to walk across, picnic areas and two playgrounds. A teenage area with a rebound wall, basketball court and 5-a-side pitch has recently been added.

A3 *Schools* — **BBONT,** the Wildlife Trust for Berks, Bucks & Oxon, Haydon Mill, Rabans Lane, **Aylesbury,** manages 32 reserves in Bucks. 01865 775476.

Schools
Open all year — **Bernwood Forest Nature Reserve** between **Oakley** and **Stanton St. John,** is a Site of Special Scientific Interest. Follow the Butterfly Trail and see how many of the 40 species breeding here you can spot. *Open daily.* 01296 625825.

Open all year — **Blackberry Farm Animal Centre,** Quainton has recently been opened by the RSPCA to care for unwanted animals. *Viewing times: 11am-4pm, daily, except Wed.* 01296 655073.

Brill Windmill, Windmill Street, is on the edge of a pretty village with lovely views. There is a large common which is ideal for picnics, walks and kite flying.

Schools
Open all year — **Buckinghamshire County Museum & Art Gallery,** Church St, **Aylesbury,** was joint winner of The National Heritage Museum of the Year Award. A wonderful museum to visit with something to interest all ages. Find out how Bucks bricks were made by hand and see how many objects you can find on the wooden Sculpture Tree. Innovative, touchable displays allow children to find out more about the exhibits for themselves. (See entry in "Discover" chapter for the Roald Dahl Children's Gallery and Advert page 54.) *Open daily, Tues-Sat, 10am-5pm; Sun and Bank Hol Mons, 2-5pm.* 01296 331441.

Grand Union Canal. A branch of the canal connects into Aylesbury offering waterside walks. Picnic sites at Pitstone Wharf and at Three Locks, nr. Soulbury.

Open all year — **Home of Rest for Horses,** Speen Farm, Slad Lane, Nr. Lacey Green, **Princes Risborough.** Come and visit the horses, ponies and donkeys who have retired here, in this long established and caring home. Don't forget your sugar lumps and carrots. Entry for visitors is free and parties are welcome by prior arrangement as are donations to further their work. *Open daily, 2-4pm. Closed last Thurs in Jul & Christmas Day.* 01494 488464. (See Advert page 11.)

Thame to Princes Risborough Cycle Way is due to open Summer 1997 on the disused railway line. 0117 9268893.

The Rye, High Wycombe, the site of many regular events, has a large children's play area. On the south side lies the Dyke, an attractive lake with boats for hire. At its eastern end is an open air pool and tennis courts. Close by is Bassetsbury Manor where there is a putting green, a croquet green, boules and tennis courts.

West Wycombe Hill, is ideal for picnics, walking and kite flying. Car parks are available at the top and bottom of the hill.

Map Ref: Please refer to map on page 4.
Schools: Range of educational opportunities available. ● Birthday parties organised.

Schools
Open all year | **Wycombe Local History and Chair Museum,** Castle Hill House, Priory Avenue, **High Wycombe,** covers the history, crafts and industries of the district with a collection of rural furniture. Brass rubbing available, also examples of lace making. *Open Mon-Fri, 10am-5pm, Sat, 10am-1pm, 2-5pm.* 01494 421895.

 Open all year | **Higginson Park and Court Gardens Grounds,** Marlow, is adjacent to the Thames with football, cricket and putting facilities. Boat hire and moorings are available with regular steamer services during the Summer (see "Trips" chapter). The park is also the home of Marlow Regatta, in mid June.

Open all year | **Bedford Embankment Gardens and Russell Park.** The banks of the great River Ouse are landscaped to make an impressive river setting. The Park offers elegant promenades, water meadows, boating lake and bandstands.

Schools
Open all year | **Bedford Museum,** Castle Lane. Housed in a converted brewery this museum covers the archaeology, social and local history, natural history and geology of North Beds. Children's holiday activities and temporary exhibitions. *Open Tues-Sat, 11am-5pm, Sun and Bank Hol Mons, 2-5pm. Closed Good Fri and Christmas.* 01234 353323.

Schools
Open all year | **Cecil Higgins Art Gallery & Museum,** Castle Close, **Bedford.** See here a gem of a dolls house; an exact replica of Oakley House, designed and made by local children in 1921. Holiday activities. *Open Tues-Sat, 11am-5pm, Sun 2-5pm. Closed Mon (except Bank Hol Mons).* 01234 211222.

Open all year | **Harrold Odell Country Park,** Harrold. This large expanse of open country surrounds landscaped lakes in former gravel pits. The River Ouse runs through the Park. There are opportunities for walks, picnics, nature observation including a bird hide, and recreation. Visitor centre. 01234 720016.

Open all year | **Stevington Postmill** is a fine, beautifully restored, 18th century mill, off the A428 Bromham Road. For safety reasons children must be accompanied by an adult. The keys are available from the pubs in Stevington, for a returnable deposit. *Open daily, 10am-7pm, or dusk in Winter.* 01234 228671.

 Schools
Open all year | **City Discovery Centre,** Milton Keynes, is on the site of a 12th century Benedictine Priory at Bradwell Abbey. Visit the Chapel of St Mary, the medieval fish ponds and the herb garden. Learn about Milton Keynes' history. Special events run during the year including Hands on History Days. *Open daily, 9am-5pm.* Admission charges may be introduced during 1997. 01908 227229.

Open all year | **Tiddenfoot Waterside Park,** Leighton Buzzard, adjacent to The Cedars Upper School in Mentmore Road, Linslade. The 30 acres, of which eight are a small lake, offer fishing and a jogging track while nearby stables run pony trekking. The park is ideal for picnics and walks and a trail follows the Grand Union Canal.

Open all year | **Willen Lakeside Park South,** Milton Keynes, close to M1, Jn. 14, offers something for all the family. Facilities include children's play areas, fitness trail, narrow gauge railway, mini bowl, cycle hire and watersports centre. (Charges for latter activities.) *Open daily, 9.30am-dusk.* 01908 670197.

 Schools
Open all year | **Ashridge Estate,** Ringshall, Berkhamsted. Four thousand acres of open space and woodland to explore. There are numerous picnic sites, footpaths and opportunities to see fallow and muntjak deer, foxes and badgers. The rare 'edible' dormouse makes his home here. There is a Visitors Centre open in Summer months. *Open daily except Friday.* 01442 851227.

Schools
Open all year | **Berkhamsted Castle.** William the Conqueror pitched camp here, though the early Norman motte and bailey fortification has walls of a later date. *Open daily, 10am-4pm.* 01442 871737 or 01604 730320.

Map Ref: Please refer to map on page 4.
Schools: Range of educational opportunities available. ● Birthday parties organised.

Schools
Open all year
Cassiobury Park, Cassiobury Park Avenue, **Watford.** Over 190 acres of parkland, with riverside walks, canal walks and boat rides, play areas, sports facilities and picnic areas. Children up to 12 can enjoy the fun of the wonderful paddling pool complex throughout the Summer months, or ride on the miniature railway which runs at weekends. Many areas of the park are a haven for wildlife and plants. A detailed Nature Trail booklet is available for schools and individuals to guide you round the park's natural history. 01923 226400. (See Advert page 8.)

Open all year
Cheslyn Gardens, Nascot Wood Road, **Watford.** Discover Watford's own secret garden! Within Chelsyn's 3.5 acres are a varied combination of garden styles, from formal lawns and annual bedding, to the more natural beauty of woodland found beyond the rock garden, with its feature pool and stream. *Open daily (not Christmas and Boxing Day), dawn to dusk.* 01923 226400.

Coombe Hill, **Wendover,** is one of the highest viewpoints of the Chilterns with views towards Aylesbury and the woods surrounding Chequers.

Schools
Open all year
Dunstable Downs Countryside Park, **Dunstable.** A park with routes and trails and a countryside centre with educational facilities and gifts for sale. Refreshments available. *Open daily.* 01582 608489.

Open all year
Ebury Way. The cycle track along this disused railway line from Watford to Rickmansworth, is a delight to cyclists and walkers alike. Spot the grebes, herons and kingfishers round the lakes and canal.

Open all year
Gadebridge Park, **Hemel Hempstead.** This town park has swings, slides and a multi-climbing frame - on a safety surface. Toddler play equipment has been newly installed. Chess, draughts, a rebuilt crazy golf, putting, petanque, croquet and a paddling pool are also in the park. Good starting point for Gade Valley Nature Trail.

Schools
Open all year
Herts & Middlesex Wildlife Trust, Grebe House, St. Michaels St., **St. Albans.** In Verulamium Park, close to the museum, this Centre has displays illustrating wildlife in the area and a wildlife garden. *Open Mar-Oct, Mon-Sat, 10am-5pm, Sun, 12-5pm. Nov-Dec, Mon-Sat, 10am-4pm & Sun, 12-4pm. Jan-Feb, Sat, 10am-4pm, & Sun, 12-4pm. Closed Christmas, New Year.* 01727 858901.

Ivinghoe Beacon, off the B489, is well worth a walk. Lovely views across surrounding countryside and car parking is conveniently close to the top of the hill.

Schools
Open all year
The John Dony Field Centre, Luton, at the heart of the Bushmead Estate, features natural history displays. *Open daily, Mon-Sat, 9.30am-5pm, Sun, 9.30am-1pm.* 01582 486983.

Schools
Open all year
Luton Museum and Art Gallery, Wardown Park, houses a fascinating Childhood Gallery. There is a collection of lace and lacemaking implements and a reconstructed 1890s Luton street scene. Other exhibits illustrate geology and natural history. *Open daily, 10am-5pm.* 01582 746722.

Open all year
The Mossman Collection, Luton, in Stockwood Park, is the largest collection of horse-drawn vehicles in Britain including the only remaining example of a Royal Mail coach. Imagine life before the railway and motor car. Horse-drawn carriage rides run daily. *(Opening times as Stockwood Museum.)* 01582 38714.

Schools
Open all year
Museum of St. Albans, Hatfield Road, tells the story of historic St. Albans from the departure of the Romans to the present day. The gallery contains the renowned Salaman collection of trade and craft tools. *Open Mon-Sat, 10am-5pm; Sun, 2-5pm.* 01727 819340.

Open all year
Stockwood Country Park, Luton, has a Craft Museum and craft workshops, playground on a safety surface with swings, climbing frame and slides. There is also an athletic track, an 18-hole public golf course and stables.

Schools
Open all year
Stockwood Craft Museum and Gardens, Farley Hill, **Luton,** in the middle of Stockwood Country Park. See a reconstruction of a thatched cottage and a working old forge. See the giant Draughts Board, period walled garden and working

Map Ref: Please refer to map on page 4.
Schools: Range of educational opportunities available. ● Birthday parties organised.

Kids bored?

They're not in Watford

Watford Leisure Centre - Horseshoe Lane, Garston

Indoor facilities and outdoor sports at Woodside Stadium. Junior courses, holiday fun sessions and much more! Call 01923 670644.

The Bill Everett Centre - Leggatts Way, Watford

Swimming and sports - "Fun House" sessions - courses and lessons - great fun for all the family. Call 01923 441444.

Watford Museum - 194 Lower High Street, Watford

Full educational service. FREE admission. Look out for the kids' holiday entertainment, street theatre, and School's Out programme. Call 01923 232297/213971.

Watford Springs - Lower High Street, Watford

Endless fun for kids of all ages - beach pool, flumes, kiddies' harbour, 25m pool and creche. Call 01923 211333.

Watford Central Baths - Hempstead Road, Watford

Traditional indoor heated pool - courses and lessons - Saturday Pirates and Parrots fun sessions. Call 01923 234636.

Cassiobury Park

Parkland, play equipment, paddling pools, miniature railway at weekends, Grand Union Canal. Fun for FREE. Call 01923 226400.

Whippendell Woods - Rousebarn Lane

Explore the ancient woodland in this hide and seek paradise. Call 01923 226400 for Nature Trail and Orienteering guides.

Fun Factory - (by the Market) Charter Place, Watford

Drop off the kids while you shop in peace! Call 01923 240964.

Sports and Play Schemes

Holiday programmes and drop-in sessions for local children. Call 01923 226400.

For general information about recreation in Watford, call the Council on 01923 226400 and ask for "Leisure".

Watford COUNCIL

bee hives. *Open Apr-Oct, Tues-Sat, 10am-5pm, Sun, 10am-6pm; Nov-Mar, Sat-Sun only 10am-4pm.* 01582 38714.

Open all year **Verulamium Park,** St. Michaels, **St. Albans,** has the remains of Roman Walls, the hypocaust and the site of the London gate to the city. A paddling pool and lake make an ideal picnic setting or enjoy the fun fair on Summer days.

Open all year **Wardown Park,** Old Bedford Road, **Luton.** A town park with swings, roundabout, climbing frame, horse and other equipment on a safety surface. There is pitch and putt, crazy golf, tennis and boating on the lake. The park is also home to Luton Museum and Art Gallery.

Schools
Open all year **Watford Museum,** 194 Lower High Street, contains something of interest for everyone. There are special Fun Days during the school holidays and a full educational service is available. There is a varied programme of temporary exhibits throughout the year, many with multicultural themes to reflect the life of the town. Exhibits chart the history of Watford from very early times up to the present day and include the printing and brewing industries. The Museum is home to a wonderful collection of art and sculpture, which sits beside more contemporary items such as Elton John's Watford Football Club stage costume. *Open Mon-Fri, 10am-5pm; Sat, 10am-1pm and 2-5pm.* 01923 232297. (See Advert page 8.)

Schools
Open all year **Wendover Woodland Park,** Upper Icknield Way, has an adventure play area and fitness "All Ability" and "Firecrest" Trails with superb views across the Aylesbury Vale. Car Parking charges. 01296 625825.

Schools
Open all year **Whippendell Woods,** Grove Mill Lane, **Watford.** 162 acres of ancient woodland and a diversity of plant and animal life, this is a great place for exploring and tracking down nature. A Nature Trail booklet and orienteering map are available from Watford Council Leisure at a nominal charge. 01923 226400.

Schools
Open all year **Black Park Country Park,** Wexham. This huge Park has areas for horse riding, walking, fishing, model boating, canoeing and swimming. There is an Information Centre, and permanent orienteering course, sensory trails and a Children's Adventure Trail. *Open daily, 8am-dusk.* 01753 511060. Car Parking charges.

Open all year **Denham Country Park.** Signposted off Jn. 1, M40, the park has wetland features being bounded by the Grand Union Canal and Colne and Misbourne rivers. Try letting your children guide you around the "Coot Trail". 01895 835852.

Open all year **Langley Park Country Park,** Wexham, on A412. Over a hundred acres of woods and parkland. Areas available for walking, cycling and horse riding. *Open daily, 8am-dusk.* 01753 511060.

Open all year **Rickmansworth Aquadrome.** Signposted from the town centre, this relaxing facility lies beside the Grand Union Canal. Among the acres of water and woodland is a good children's playground and opportunities for fishing, sailing and windsurfing. (See Watersports in "Activities" chapter and Advert page 23.) *Open Apr-Aug, 8am-8pm; Sept-Mar, 8am-dusk.*

Schools
Open all year **First Garden City Heritage Museum,** Norton Way South, Letchworth. Displays show the social history of Letchworth and the founding of the Garden City Movement with computer touch screen displays. *Open Mon-Sat, 10am-5pm.* 01462 482710. (Possible closure for redevelopment during 1997).

Schools
Open all year **Letchworth Museum,** The Broadway, concentrates on art, archaeology and local natural history. Lots of events and exhibitions for children of all ages are held. *Open Mon-Sat, 10am-5pm.* 01462 685647.

Open all year **Wood Green Animal Shelters,** King's Bush Farm, **Godmanchester,** (just off A14). There are lots of rescued animals to see including cats, dogs, goats, sheep, llamas, Vietnamese pigs and many other unusual animals. Youngsters can join The Junior Supporters or Critters Club. *Open daily, 9am-3pm.* 01480 830014.

Map Ref: Please refer to map on page 4.
Schools: Range of educational opportunities available. ● Birthday parties organised.

Open all year **Wood Green Animal Shelters,** Chishill Road, Heydon, near **Royston.** Visit the cats and other animals including rabbits and guinea pigs. Youngsters can join The Junior Supporters or Critters Club. *Open daily, 9am-3pm.* 01763 838329.

 Open all year **Aldenham Country Park,** Aldenham Road, **Elstree.** 175 acres of woodland and parkland surrounded by a large reservoir. Extensive footpath network, a rare breeds centre, lakeside fishing and small adventure playground. Refreshments available. *Open daily, Summer 9am-6pm, Winter 9am-4pm.* 0181 953 9602.

Open all year **Castle Gardens & Sworders Field,** Bishops Stortford. A very pleasant spot with the River Stort running through its centre. There is a children's paddling pool, tennis courts and a playground with a variety of play equipment.

Open all year **Cheshunt Park.** 126 acres of open space and woodland, full of history with evidence of Roman occupation. It has many species of plants and animals and is a birdwatcher's paradise. Many golfing facilities.

Schools *Open all year* **Fairlands Valley Park,** Six Hills Way, **Stevenage.** Over 120 acres in the centre of Stevenage includes an 11 acre lake used for sailing and windsurfing throughout the year. There is a children's boating lake with a Dragon boat, play area, three mini-paddling pools and an orienteering course and cafe. *Children's boating lake opens daily through the school Summer hols.* 01438 353241.

Open all year **Hartham Common,** Hertford. Beside the river you will find an indoor swimming pool and putting green, pitch and putt, tennis, routabout, Trim Trail, and a play area with swings, a see-saw, climbing frame, swing bridge and balancing beams on an impact resistant surface.

Hertford Castle. Near the town centre, the Castle is open on the first Sunday of the summer months when local councillors are in attendance to guide visitors around. Brass band concerts in the castle grounds from 2.30pm. Adjoining the Castle is a playground. *Open May-Sept, 2.30-4.30pm. Grounds open all year, daily.* 01992 584322.

Schools *Open all year* **Hertford Museum,** Bull Plain, houses a penny farthing cycle and two fine dolls houses side by side, besides curiosities such as the skin of a boa constrictor and the armour of a Japanese Samurai Warrior. Many other exhibits from the area cover social history, natural history, geology and archaeology. See the Jacobean garden, with a knot garden, arbour and turf seat. *Open Tues-Sat, 10am-5pm.* 01992 582686.

Schools *Open all year* **Hitchin Museum and Art Gallery,** Paynes Park. Many interesting exhibits connected with the town, its market and industries. See the old chemist's shop and medicinal plant garden. Holiday activities. *Open Mon-Sat, 10am-5pm, Sun, 2-4.30pm. Closed Bank Hol Mons.* 01462 434476.

Open all year **Lee Valley Park Countryside Centre,** Waltham Abbey, located in the Abbey Gardens, has a local history exhibition and lots of other information on the Park. *Open daily, 10am-5pm; 10.30am-4pm in Winter.* 01992 713838.

Open all year **Lee Valley Regional Park,** stretches along the River Lee, from London to Hertfordshire. Take a picnic and explore the woodlands and water margins for wildlife. A day out for all the family with boat trips, farm visits and sporting activities. Visit the Countryside Centre (above) for information. 01992 713838.

Schools *Open all year* **Lowewood Museum,** High Street, **Hoddesdon,** has three galleries, two of which contain permanent displays of pictures and artefacts. The third has a varied programme of changing displays. Children's workshops and activities are organised. *Open Wed and Sat, 10am-4pm.* 01992 445596. (See Advert page 18.)

Schools *Open all year* **Mill Green Mill,** Mill Green, **Hatfield.** Next door to the Mill Green Museum, this recently renovated mill, rebuilt in 1762, stands on the River Lee. There are viewing galleries on each floor. Flour is milled every week, weather and demand for flour permitting, and is on sale. Can be noisy. *Open Tues-Fri, 10am-5pm. Sat, Sun, Bank Hol Mons, 2-5pm.* 01707 271362. (See Advert page 12.)

Map Ref: Please refer to map on page 4.
Schools: Range of educational opportunities available. ● Birthday parties organised.

C3 Schools / Open all year — **Mill Green Museum,** Mill Green, **Hatfield.** This attractive museum concentrates on artefacts and exhibits of local interest with a changing programme of temporary exhibitions. Find out about Iron Age chieftains, a Roman skeleton and the District's railways. During the Summer experts demonstrate crafts and skills at weekends. Don't miss the Mill next door, phone for milling times. *Open Tues-Fri, 10am-5pm, Sat, Sun and Bank Hol Mons, 2-5pm.* 01707 271362. (See Advert page 12.)

Open all year — **Northaw Great Wood,** Cuffley. Specially marked walks plus picnic areas and visitors information centre.

Open all year — **Priory Gardens,** Ware. Lawns and public gardens, plus a 'Fishermans Walk' along the River Lee to the lock close by. Children's play area, outdoor heated swimming pool, toddlers pool and tennis courts. 01920 460316.

Open all year — **RSPCA Animal Centre,** Southridge, Packhorse Lane, **Ridge,** near South Mimms on the M25. Not only can you give unwanted, neglected and abandoned animals a good home but you can also see birds, goats and rabbits. No charge but a donation would be appreciated. *Open Mon-Sat, 11am-4.30pm, Suns and Bank Hol Mons, 1-4.30pm. Closed Weds.* 01707 642153.

Open all year — **Stanborough Park,** Stanborough Rd, **Welwyn Garden City.** The Park is an attractive countryside facility which includes a boating and canoeing lake, sailing and windsurfing and model boat lake. Also within the park is Stanborough Splashland outdoor swimming complex with water slides and a sandpit area. There is a crazy golf course, children's play area and lakeside cafe. (See "Activities" chapter.) 01707 327655. (See Advert page 12.)

Schools / Open all year — **Stevenage Museum,** St. George's Way. Videos depict the story of the town's development. Try your hand at designing a new town in one of the computer quizzes available. Holiday activities and family events organised. *Open Mon-Sat, 10am-5pm. Closed Bank Hol Mons.* 01438 354292.

Spend a day

in *Welwyn Garden City* and *Hatfield*

Leisure
WELWYN HATFIELD COUNCIL

ROLLERCITY
Tel: (01707) 332880
- *Family sessions* • *Free skate hire*
- *Rollerdiscos* • *Skate lessons*

HATFIELD SWIM CENTRE
Tel: (01707) 264487
- *Family Sessions* • *Junior fun afternoons*
- *Swimming lessons* • *Creche available*

WELWYN ROMAN BATHS
Tel: (01707) 271362
- *Roman baths under A1 (M)*
- *A fascinating insight into how the Romans took a bath*

HATFIELD LEISURE CENTRE
Tel: (01707) 268769
- *Courses for children* • *Special holiday sessions* • *Creche available*

PANSHANGER GOLF
Tel: (01707) 333312
- *Pitch & Putt* • *Junior Golf Lessons*

SPLASHLAND
Tel: (01707) 322833 or (01707) 264487
- *Open air pool with water slides*
- *Learner pool, paddling pools*
- *Huge sandy play areas*

MILL GREEN MUSEUM & MILL
Tel: (01707) 271362
- *18th Century working water mill*
- *Exhibitions of local history & crafts*
- *Phone to check opening and milling times*

STANBOROUGH PARK
Tel: (01707) 327655
- *Sailing lake and boating lake*
- *Crazy golf*
- *Nature Trail*
- *Fishing*
- *Windsurfing & sailing school*
- *Childrens playground*

*AND DON'T FORGET... We also have children's films and entertainment at Campus West Theatre in Welwyn Garden City **(01707) 332880** and at the Forum Entertainment Centre in Hatfield **(01707) 271217**. Playschemes are run throughout the District during the school holidays, **Tel: (01707) 357150** for details.*

ACTIVITIES
& INFORMATION DIRECTORY

CONTENTS

General abbreviations used in addresses within the listings are as follows: Ave.: Avenue, Clo.: Close, Cresc.: Crescent, Dri.: Drive, Gdns.: Gardens, Gr.: Green, Gro.: Grove, La.: Lane, Pk.: Park, Pl.: Place, R.G.: Recreation Ground, Rd.: Road, Sq.: Square, St.: Street, Tce.: Terrace.

✦: Birthday Party

Abbreviations specific to a particular section are listed at the beginning of that section.

BOAT HIRE

Abbreviations: C: Canoes, M: Motor boats, P: Pedalos, R: Rowing boats.

MAP REFS

A3 **High Wycombe,** The Rye. R.

A4 **Marlow,** Higginson Pk. R.

B1 **Bedford,** Longholme Boating Lake. *Open Easter-Oct, daily, 10am-6pm.* 01234 215607. C. P. R.

B2 **Milton Keynes,** Willen Lake and Pk. C.

B3 **Luton,** Wardown Pk. R.

A3 **Broxbourne,** Lee Valley Boat Centre. M.R. Day boats and 6-berth narrow-boats. 01992 462085.
Stevenage, Fairlands Valley Park. C.P.R. 01438 353241.

MAP REFS

A3 **Welwyn Garden City.** Stanborough Pk. C. P. R.

BOWLING (TEN PIN)

An increasingly popular activity providing fun for a family outing. Many centres have bumper lanes and lightweight bowls enabling youngsters to enjoy this sport.

A3 **Aylesbury,** Jardines Club, Friars Sq. Shopping Centre. 01296 415698.

B1 ✦ **Bedford,** Megabowl, Aspects Leisure Pk. 01234 271717.

B2 ✦ **Milton Keynes,** MK Super Bowl, Leisure Plaza, South Row. 01908 231400. **Rollers UK,** Denbigh North Leisure, 01908 366448.

B3 ✦ **Dunstable,** Megabowl, Court Dri. 01582 472727.
✦ **Hemel Hempstead,** Hot Shots, Jarman Park. 01442 292208.

✦ **Watford,** Hollywood Bowl, Woodside Leisure Park, Garston. 01923 682929.

C3 ✦ **Stevenage,** Megabowl, Roaring Meg Retail Park. 01438 355522.

BRASS RUBBING

A3 **High Wycombe,** Wycombe Local History and Chair Museum. 01494 421895. (See "Fun for Free" chapter.)

B3 **St Albans,** St Albans Cathedral. (See "Discover" chapter.)

CINEMAS

A3 **Aylesbury,** Odeon, Cambridge St. 01296 339588/82660.
High Wycombe, UCI Wycombe 6, Crest Rd. 01494 463333/0900 888990.

B1 **Bedford,** Virgin Cinema, Aspects Leisure Pk., Newnham Ave. 01234 266344.
Milton Keynes, The Point 10, 602 Midsummer Boulevard. 01908 661662.

B3 **Chesham,** The Elgiva, Elgiva La. 01494 774759.
Gerrards Cross, ABC, Elthorpe Cresc. 01753 882516/883024.

B3 **Hemel Hempstead,** Odeon, Jarman Park. 01442 292210.
Luton, ABC, 51 George St. 01582 22537.

Map Ref: Please refer to map on page 4. ✦ Birthday parties organised.

13

ACTIVITIES

B3 **Watford**, ABC, Merton Rd. 01923 233259. **Warners**, Woodside Leisure Park, Garston. 01923 682222.

B4 **Beaconsfield**, The Beacon Centre, Hotspur Way. 01494 677764.

C2 **Letchworth**, Broadway Cinema, Eastcheap. 01462 681223.

Royston, Priory Cinema, Newmarket Rd. 01763 243133.

C3 **Broxbourne**, Broxbourne Civic Hall, High St. 01992 441946.

Hatfield, UCI 9 Cinema, The Galleria. 01707 270222.

Potters Bar, Wyllyotts Centre, Wyllyotts Pl., Darke La. 01707 645005.

Stevenage, Cineworld, Leisure Park. 01438 740944.

Welwyn Garden City, Campus West Theatre. 01707 332880.

CRAZY GOLF

B3 **Hemel Hempstead**, Gadebridge Pk.

Luton, Wardown Pk.

St. Albans, Verulamium Pk.

C3 **Welwyn Garden City**, Stanborough Pk.

CYCLING & BMX

C3 **Cheshunt**, Herts Young Mariners Base, Windmill La. Mountain bikes. 01992 628403.

Welwyn Garden City, Gosling Sports Pk. 01707 331056.

C4 Eastway Cycle Centre, Temple Mills La., London E15. 0181 534 6085.

DAY CAMPS

B1 **Bedford**, The Outdoor Centre, Hillgrounds Rd., Kempston. This Bedfordshire County Council run facility offers day, evening, weekend and residential opportunities for young people and adults. Home to probably the best indoor climbing facility in the region, the centre also offers canoeing, kayaking and archery facilities. Excellent equipment and instruction available with some sections which can be used towards the Duke of Edinburgh Award Scheme. 01234 854959. (See Advert page 14.)

B3 Camp Energy, 01923 662224 / 01582 767722.

PACT Day Camps. 01442 872859.

FAMILY ENTERTAINMENT CENTRES

Abbreviations: C: Cinema, F.P.: Fun Park, L: Laser Games, P: Pool, S: Skating, T: Ten Pin Bowling.

B3 **Hemel Hempstead**, Jarman Pk. C, F.P., P, S, T.

Watford, Woodside Leisure Pk. C, F.P., S, T.

ICE SKATING

B2 ✦ **Milton Keynes**, Blade Runner, MK Leisure Plaza, 1 South Row, Child's Way H6. 01908 696696.

B3 ✦ **Hemel Hempstead**, Silver Blades, Jarman Pk. 01442 292202.

✦ **Watford**, Woodside Leisure Pk., Garston. 01923 663463.

C4 ✦ **Leyton, London**, Lee Valley Ice Centre, Lee Bridge Rd., E10. 0181 533 3155.

KARTING & QUAD BIKES

A2 ✦ **Water Stratford**, Armco Quads & Karts, Grands Farm, Nr. Buckingham. 01280 703625/812327.

B2 ✦ **Milton Keynes**, Magna Karta. Bletcham Way. 01908 644844.

B3 ✦ **St. Albans**, Karting Challenge Co., free parking/access via Bowman's Farm overflow car park. An off-road karting and Quad Bike Centre for children of all ages. Karts available for children from 3 to 12+. Special bookings for parties, families and groups or just arrive and drive at weekends and school holidays. Great fun for all the family. 01707 263505. (See Advert page 14.)

C3 ✦ **Hoddesdon**, Kart Raceway, Rye House Stadium, Rye Rd. 01992 451170.

LASER CHALLENGE

A3 ✦ **High Wycombe**, Quasar, Oxford St. 01494 441011.

B1 ✦ **Bedford**, Zapp Zone, Aspects Leisure Pk. 01234 269037.

✦ **Milton Keynes**, Quasar, Leisure Plaza, South Row. 01908 231400.

B3 ✦ **Hemel Hempstead**, Quasar, 179 The Marlowes. 4 scenes in one arena! 01442 213200.

✦ **St. Albans**, Laser Zone, (at London Colney R.C.) *Tues-Thurs 6-9pm*. Bookings only, 01727 822447.

B3 ✦ **Watford**, Amazone, Laser Quest, The Parade. 01923 222223.

Map Ref: Please refer to map on page 4. ✦ Birthday parties organised.

15

ACTIVITIES

C3 ✦ **Stevenage**, Quasar, Old Stevenage Bowl, Dane St. 01438 748263.

PADDLING POOLS

These can be great fun for younger children on hot days and are usually free.

B3 **Bushey**, King George Recreation Ground.

Hemel Hempstead, Gadebridge Pk.

St Albans, Verulamium Pk.

Watford, Cassiobury Pk.

C3 **Bishops Stortford**, Castle Gdns.

Stevenage, Fairlands Valley Pk.

PITCH & PUTT

A3 **Aylesbury**, Bedgrove & Alfred Rose Pks.

High Wycombe, Wycombe Heights Golf Centre, Rayners Ave. 01494 816686.

B1 **Emberton**, Emberton Country Pk. (Apr-Oct).

B2 **Milton Keynes**, Mount Farm Pk.

B3 **Harpenden**, Rothampstead Pk.

Luton, Wardown Pk.

Watford, Cassiobury Pk.

B4 **Rickmansworth**, Rickmansworth Golf Course.

C3 **Hertford**, Hartham Common.

Stevenage, Hampson Pk.

Welwyn Garden City, Panshanger Golf Course, Herns La.

PUTTING GREENS

A3 **High Wycombe**, Bassetsbury Manor.

A4 **Marlow**, Higginson Pk.

B1 **Emberton**, Emberton Country Pk. (Apr-Oct).

B2 **Milton Keynes**, Windmill Hills, Standing Way and Abbey Hill.

B3 **Hemel Hempstead**, Gadebridge Pk.

Luton, Stockwood Park Golf Course.

St. Albans, Batchwood Pk and Clarence Pk.

C2 **Letchworth**, Norton Common and Howard Gdns.

C3 **Baldock**, Avenue Pk.

Cheshunt, Cheshunt Pk, Park La.

Hertford, Hartham Common.

Hoddesdon, Rye Park Recreation Ground, Rye Rd.

Stevenage, Hampson Pk, King George V Pk, St. Nicholas Pk and Shepalbury Pk.

Ware, Priory Gdns.

Welwyn Garden City, Panshanger Golf Course, Herns La.

ROLLER SKATING

Roller skating is often also on offer at Sports Centres.

B2 ✦ **Milton Keynes**, Rollers, Denbigh North Leisure. 01908 366440.

B3 ✦ **Bushey**, Hartspring SLC, Park Ave., 01923 233039. (To close for 12 months May 1997).

C3 ✦ **Welwyn Garden City**, Rollercity, Campus West. 01707 332880. (See Advert page 12.)

SNOWSPORTS

A3 ✦ **High Wycombe**, Wycombe Summit, Abbey Barn Lane, is set in 70 acres of beautiful woodland, between Jns 3 & 4 of the M40, and has the longest ski slope in England. The redesigned 300m Dendix main slope, a 100m trainer slope, nursery areas, three lifts and full misting system offer superb facilities for both skiers and boarders. The highly qualified international ski & snowboard instructors have access to new state of the art video coaching equipment. The latest timing equipment means that Wycombe Summit is a National race location. The log cabin "Retreat" cafe/bar offers a chance to relax and enjoy some Apres-Ski. There is also a function room available for bookings and a health and fitness suite. *Open daily, 10am-10pm.* 01494 474711. (See Advert page 20.)

B3 ✦ **Hemel Hempstead**, Hemel Ski Centre, St. Albans Hill, just off M1 Jn 8 and links to M25 and M10, has a large main slope, wave run, trainer slope and three ski lifts. In addition to recreational skiing and snow boarding, private lesson or group tuition is available from fully qualified instructors. Children's courses and racing camps are held during school holidays. Eight levels of junior activities are available on Saturday mornings, working towards British Alpine Ski Awards. Children's parties can include skiing and tobogganning, with an apres-ski bar and well stocked ski shop. Hemel Ski Centre offers super facilities for all the family. *Open daily.* 01442 241321. (See Advert page 14.)

Map Ref: Please refer to map on page 4.   ✦ Birthday parties organised.

16

C3 ✦ **Welwyn Garden City,** Gosling **Sports Pk.,** Stanborough Rd. One of the many facilities at this excellent sports complex is a dry ski-slope, with tuition by qualified instructors available for skiers at all levels, including a kindergarten and a gentle nursery slope for beginners. The cafe/bar is also excellent for a little apres-ski relaxation. (See Advert page 20.)

SPORT, FUN & PLAYSCHEMES

B3 **Watford.** The Council provides a full programme of activities for local young people, including holiday Play schemes for 5-11 year olds and free youth drop-in sessions for 11-16 year olds. For those interested in learning or improving sporting skills, there is the Sportsworld scheme which includes exciting Summer camps for full-time fun. 01923 226400. (See Advert page 8.)

Welwyn/Hatfield. The Leisure Department offers a varied programme of playschemes through the Easter and Summer school holidays. Courses range from juggling to horse riding! 01707 357150. (See Advert page 12.)

Gosling Sports Park. Sport and activity sessions are available during term-time in addition to holiday courses and workshops, ranging from gymnastics and football to bouncy castle and face-painting. (See Advert page 20.)

C3 **Borough of Broxbourne.** Summer Fun. Join in the Summer fun and be involved in playschemes, workshops, organised sports activities, a playbus for under 5s, puppet shows, Teddy Bears' picnics, day trips and much more for children of all ages. For your free copy of the Borough of Broxbourne Summer Leisure Guide telephone 01992 785546. (See Advert page 18.)

SPORTS & LEISURE CENTRES

Abbreviations: LC: Leisure Centre, RC: Recreation Centre, SC: Sports Centre, SH: Sports Hall.

*Centre has an indoor swimming pool.

A2 **Buckingham,** The Swan Pool & LC*, London Rd. 01280 817500.

Winslow, Winslow Centre, Park Rd.,01296 555210/714335.

A3 ✦ **High Wycombe,** Wycombe SC*, Marlow Hill. 01494 446324.

A4 ✦ **Marlow,** Court Gdns, Pound La. 01628 898080.

B1 ✦ **Bedford,** Bedford Athletic Stadium, Barkers La. 01234 351115. Bunyan Centre, Mile Rd. 01234 364481.

B2 ✦ **Bletchley,** Bletchley LC*, Princes Way. 01908 377251.

✦ **Flitwick,** SLC*, Steppingley Rd. 01525 717744.

✦ **Leighton Buzzard,** Tiddenfoot LC*, Mentmore Rd, Linslade. 01525 375765. **Milton Keynes,** Shenley LC*. 01908 502488. Stantonbury Campus LC. 01908 314466. Woughton LC*, Rainbow Dri., Leadenhall, 01908 660392.

B3 ✦ **Berkhamsted,** SC*, Douglas Gdns., has a wide range of activities for children. Instructors provide quality coaching to encourage all abilities to enjoy exercise in a friendly atmosphere. Roller skating, badminton, trampoline, soccer and kinder gym are available on the dryside. Canoe club, swimming lessons, rookie lifeguard, lifesaving, babysplash and tadpoles are just a few of the waterbased activities. Phone 01442 877855 for an information pack. (See Advert page 18.)

✦ **Bricket Wood,** SC*, Smug Oak La. 01923 662224.

✦ **Bushey,** Hartspring SLC, Park Ave. 01923 233039. (*To close for one year May 1997*).

✦ **Chesham,** Chesham LC*, White Hill. 01494 791777.

✦ **Dunstable,** LC*, Court Drive, run a special high standard Gym School and Swim School. 01582 608107. (See also "Swimming" and Advert page 44.)

Harpenden, SC*, Rothampstead Pk., Leyton Rd. 01582 767722.

Map Ref: Please refer to map on page 4. ✦ Birthday parties organised.

17

THERE'S SO MUCH TO DO IT'S BROXBOURNE AGAIN AND AGAIN AND AGAIN

BOROUGH OF BROXBOURNE

There's holiday and half term capers and a fun-filled, action packed Summer Leisure Programme. Themed events, sports courses, arts and crafts workshops, day trips, playschemes and 'come & try' days are all on offer with activities ranging from Scuba Diving to Teddy Bear's Picnics.

To find our more join the free mailing list quoting the age of your children. Telephone 01992 785555 extn 5906.

DACORUM BOROUGH COUNCIL

KID'S STUFF ...

DACORUM

- **P**AVGANG **K**IDS **C**LUB
- **Y**EAR ROUND ACTIVITIES
- **S**UMMER **P**LAYSCHEMES
- **A**DVENTURE **P**LAYGROUNDS
- **H**OLIDAY **S**PECIALS AT **S**PORTS **C**ENTRES
- **O**LD **T**OWN **H**ALL **C**HILDREN'S **T**HEATRE

FOR INFORMATION ON THINGS TO DO WITH THE KIDS IN HEMEL HEMPSTEAD, BERKHAMSTED, TRING AND SURROUNDING AREA, CALL

01442 234222

18

MAP REFS

B3 ✦ **Hemel Hempstead**, Dacorum SC*, Park Rd., is undergoing major refurbishment. Many activities are relocated during period of closure. Please call the Centre for details. 01442 64822. (See Advert page 18.)

Houghton Regis, LC*, Houghton Regis Upper School. 01582 866141.

✦ **London Colney**, RC, Alexander Rd. 01727 822447.

✦ **Luton**, High Town RC, 34-38 Old Bedford Rd. 01582 36753. **Lea Manor RC***, Northwell Dr. 01582 599888. **Luton**

✦ **Regional SC**, St. Thomas's Rd. 01582 416772.

✦ **Redbourn**, RC, 75 Dunstable Rd. 01582 626202.

✦ **Rickmansworth**, William Penn LC*, Mill End, Shepherds La. 01923 771050.

St. Albans, Batchwood Tennis and ✦**Golf Centre**. 01727 844250. **Westminster Lodge LC***, Holywell Hill. 01727 846031.

✦ **Stopsley**, Putteridge RC*, Putteridge Rd. 01582 31664.

Tring, Tring SC*, Mortimer Hill. Opens to the public during evenings and weekends during term times, and all week during school holidays. For details of opening hours and activities call 01442 822353. (See Advert page 18.)

✦ **Watford**, The Bill Everett Centre*, Leggatts Way, is an ideal facility combining a swimming pool, sports hall and community hall. Special 'Fun House' sessions and children's workshops are held at Easter and in the Summer. Swimming lessons and sports courses are held throughout the year. 01923 4414444. (See Advert page 8.)

✦ **Watford LC**, Horseshoe Lane, Garston, has a wide range of activities for children, allowing them to progress in their chosen sport whilst having fun. There are programmed courses and facilities for a wide range of individual sports, including squash, snooker, gymnastics, badminton and football. Woodside Stadium, adjacent to the Centre, is one of the top athletic venues in the area and courses are available to start or improve skills. 01923 670644. (See Advert page 8.)

B4 ✦ **Beaconsfield**, The Beacon Centre, Holtspur Way. 01494 677764. **Chalfont St. Peter**, Chalfont LC*, Nicol Rd. 01753 888444.

✦ **Iver**, Evreham SC, Swallow St. 01753 672610.

C2 ✦ **Biggleswade**, RC, Eagle Farm Rd. 01767 315651.

Letchworth, Fearnhill SC, Icknield Way. 01462 676017.

✦ **North Herts** LC*, Baldock Rd. 01462 679723.

C3 ✦ **Cheshunt**, Grundy Pk LC*, Windmill La. 01992 623345.

✦ **Hatfield**, Hatfield LC, Travellers La. For members, squash and badminton courts and all-weather pitches are available and courses are offered in various sports, including martial arts and karate. Special holiday sessions are organised. 01707 268769. (See Advert page 12.)

✦ **Hoddesdon**, John Warner SC, Stanstead Rd. 01992 445375.

Potters Bar, Furzefield Centre*, Mutton La. 01707 657026. *(Re-opening March 1997).*

✦ **Stevenage**, Arts & LC, Lytton Way. 01438 766877. **John Henry Newman LC**, Hitchin Rd. 01438 741511.

✦ **Ware**, Wodson Pk SC, Wadesmill Rd. 01920 487091.

✦ **Welwyn Garden City**, Gosling Sports Pk, Stanborough Rd. Multi sports complex including dry ski slope with kindergarten, 18 indoor/outdoor tennis courts, football, athletics, bars and cafe. A wide range of sport and activity sessions during term-time are available in addition to holiday courses and workshops from trampolining to bouncy castle. Just outside Welwyn Garden City, off Jn 4 A1/(M) and close to both the M25 and M1. *Open all year, 9am-11pm.* 01707 331056. (See Advert page 20.)

SWIMMING POOLS (INDOOR)

Please also check the list of Sports & Leisure Centres above. Those marked with an * have a pool.

A2 ✦ **Buckingham**, Swan Pool & LC*, London Rd. 01280 817500.

A3 **Aylesbury**, Reg Maxwell Pools, Exchange St. 01296 555550.

ACTIVITIES

Map Ref: Please refer to map on page 4. ✦ Birthday parties organised.

19

A3 **Princes Risborough**, Risborough Springs, Wades Pk. 01844 274200.

B1 **Bedford**, Kempston Pool, Hillgrounds Leisure, Hillgrounds Rd. 01234 843777. Robinson Pool, Bedford Park, Park Ave. 01234 354901.

B2 **Milton Keynes**, Woughton Campus, Rainbow Dri., Leadenhall. 01908 660392. **Newport Pagnell**, Middleton Pool, Tickford St. 01908 610477.

B3 ✦**Amersham**, The Chiltern Pools, Chiltern Ave. 01494 433061.
Buntingford, Ward Freman Pool, Bowling Green La. 01763 272566.
Bushey, Bushey Hall Pool, Falconer Rd. 0181 950 6497.

Dunstable LC, Court Dri, runs a swim school dedicated to providing a Teacher Centre of Excellence. All ages and abilities are catered for with Award schemes to promote the highest standards of technique. 01582 608107. (See Advert page 44.)

Luton, Lewsey Pool, Pastures Way, Lewsey. 01582 604244. **Wardown Swimming & LC**, Bath Rd. 01582 20621.

Watford, Central Baths, Hempstead Rd. Swimming lessons are available all year with crash courses in the school holidays. Pirates and Parrots fun sessions are run on Saturdays and during school holidays. Try out a fun-packed Sharks Activity week for 8-16 year olds. 01923 234636. (See Advert page 8.)

Watford Springs (see Water Fun Parks).

✦ **Sir James Altham Pool**, is situated in Little Oxhey La., South Oxhey. There is a warm and friendly welcome for all visitors here. The pool, 25m by 8m, slopes gently, making it ideal for lots of activities. The water temperature is maintained at 29⁰C. Highly qualified instructors give professional advice and help. *Open daily except Christmas, Boxing and New Year's Days.* 0181 421 0211. (See Advert page 20)

C2 **Biggleswade**, Playfield Clo. New pool due to open 1997. 01767 313992.

C3 **Bishops Stortford**, Grange Paddocks Pool, Rye St. 01279 652332.
Borehamwood, Hertsmere Centre Pool, Elstree Way. 0181 953 1274.
Cheshunt, Grundy Park Pool, Windmill La. 01992 623345.

✦**Hatfield**, Hatfield Swim Centre, Hatfield Town Centre has a full-length indoor pool, a learner and baby pool. A varied programme of lessons is offered plus Junior fun and family sessions. There is also a creche and a cafe overlooking the pool which offers children's meals. Other facilities include a gym, sauna, steam room, sunbeds and jacuzzi. 01707 264487. (See Advert page 12.)

Hertford, Hartham Pool, Hartham Common. 01992 583086.

✦**Hitchin**, Hitchin Swimming Centre, Fishponds Rd. 01462 441646.

C3 **Sawbridgeworth**, Leventhorpe Pool, Cambridge Rd. 01279 722490.

C3 **Stevenage**, Pool, St. Georges Way. 01438 312467. *(To close Sept. 1997 for 9 months).*
Ware, Fanshawe Pool, Park Rd. 01920 466967.

SWIMMING POOLS (OUTDOOR)

A3 **Aylesbury**, The Vale Pool, Park St. 01296 82050.

High Wycombe, Holywell Mead Pool, Battersbury La. 01494 452866.

B2 **Wolverton**, Milton Keynes, Aylesbury St. West, 01908 312091.

B3 **Chesham**, Chesham Heated Open Air Pool, The Moor. 01494 783068.

Dear Leap, Little Gaddesden, Ringshaw. 01442 842412.

Hemel Hempstead, Dacorum SC. 01442 64822.

C2 **Biggleswade**, Playfield Clo. 01767 313992.

Letchworth, Icknield Way. 01462 684673.

C3 **Royston**, Newmarket Rd. 01763 245577.

Hoddesdon, Hoddesdon Open Air Pool, High St. 01992 461592.

Ware, Priory Lido, Priory St. 01920 460703.

Welwyn Garden City, Splashland, Stanborough Pk. 01707 322833.

THEATRES

A3 **Aylesbury**, Civic Theatre, Market Sq. 01296 86009. Limelight Theatre, Queens Pk Arts Centre. 01296 24332/431272.

High Wycombe, Spring Gardens Art Centre, Pinions Rd. 01494 464800. The Swan, St. Mary's St. 01494 512000.

ACTIVITIES

Map Ref: Please refer to map on page 4. ✦ Birthday parties organised.

A4 **Marlow**, The Puppet Theatre Barge. 0836 202745.

B2 **Leighton Buzzard**, Theatre and Arts Centre, Library, Lake St. 01525 378310.

Milton Keynes, Community Arts Workshops, at **Coffee Hall**. 01908 678306. **Galley Hill**. 01908 563661. **The Courtyard and Barn Theatre**. 01908 608108. **Madcap**, St. Georges Centre, Creed St., Wolverton. 01908 320173. **The Stables**, Stockwell La., Wavendon. 01908 583928. **Stantonbury Campus Theatre**, Stantonbury. 01908 224234. **Woughton Centre**, Woughton Campus, Rainbow Drive, Leadenhall. 01908 660392.

B3 **Chesham**, Elgiva Theatre, Elgiva La. 01494 774759.

Hemel Hempstead, Dacorum Pavilion, Marlowes. Special children's shows with television favourites often run and the popular Pavgang Saturday Kids Club, offers a weekly portion of fun and entertainment for 5-12 year olds. Box Office: 01442 64451 or 234300. (See Advert page 18.)

The Old Town Hall, High St. The Children's Theatre Season offers professional theatre for 3-10 year olds. Give your children the opportunity to see live theatre from an early age at a reasonable price. 01442 242827 for details of shows and prices. (See Advert page 18.)

Luton, St. George's Theatre, third floor Central Library, St. George's Sq. 01582 21628.

St. Albans, Alban Arena, Civic Centre, St. Peters St. 01727 844488. **Maltings Arts Centre**. 01727 844222.

Watford, Watford Palace Theatre, Clarendon Rd. 01923 225671.

B4 **Beaconsfield**, The Beacon Centre, Holtspur Way. 01494 677764.

Rickmansworth, Watersmeet Theatre, Town Centre. 01923 771542.

C3 **Barnet**, The Bull, High St. 0181 449 5189.

Broxbourne, Broxbourne Civic Hall, High St. 01992 441946.

Cheshunt, Wolsey Hall, Windmill La. 01992 632812.

Hatfield, Forum, Entertainment Centre, Lemsford Rd. 01707 271217.

C3 **Hertford**, Castle Hall, The Wash. 01992 589024.

Hitchin, The Queen Mother Theatre, Woodside, Walsworth Rd. 01462 455166.

Potters Bar, Wyllyotts Centre, Wyllyotts Pl., Darke La. 01707 645005.

Stevenage, Gordon Craig Theatre, Lytton Way. 01438 766866.

Welwyn Garden City, Campus West Theatre, programme of children's workshops during holidays. 01707 332880.

WATER FUN PARKS

B1 ✦ **Bedford**, Oasis Leisure Pool, Cardington Rd. 01234 272100.

B2 ✦ **Bletchley**, Bletchley LC, Princes Way, has a flume. 01908 377251.

✦ **Milton Keynes**, Dolphin Splashdown Water Fun Centre, Shenley Church End (V4). 01908 503344.

B3 ✦ **Amersham**, The Chiltern Pools, Bensheim Way, has a fun leisure pool. 01494 586800.

✦ **Hemel Hempstead**, Aquasplash, Jarmans Field. 01442 292203.

✦ **Watford**, Watford Springs, Lower High St. This exciting leisure pool provides endless fun for children of all ages in a warm and friendly tropical paradise. Small children can play in the kiddies harbour with its friendly dolphin and pirate boat. Older children will enjoy the rapid ride, beach pool and thrills and spills of the flumes - two speeds, fast and faster! For serious swimming there is also a 25m pool. Refreshments and creche facilities are available and a full programme of swimming lessons, with crash courses during the school holidays. 01923 211333. (See Advert page 24.)

C2 **Letchworth**, North Herts LC, Baldock Rd. 01462 679311.

C3 **Welwyn Garden City**, Splashland, Stanborough Park, Stanborough Rd. An outdoor water fun complex with a wide range of features for all the family. The main pool has two giant water slides. For toddlers there is a special sandy play area, a learner and a paddling pool. *Open Apr-Sept.* 01707 322833 or 264487. (See Advert page 12.)

Map Ref: Please refer to map on page 4. ✦ Birthday parties organised.

22

WATERSPORTS

Abbreviations: C: Canoeing, JS: Jet Skiing, K: Kayaking, S: Sailing, W: Windsurfing, WS: Waterskiing.

A4 **Marlow,** Bisham Abbey Nat. Sports Centre. C. S. 01628 474960. Westthorpe Farm, JS. W. WS. 01628 486617.

B1 **Bedford, The Outdoor Centre,** Hillgrounds Rd., Kempston. An excellent facility offering tuition in canoeing and kayaking by qualified instructors from beginners to advanced levels, including a slalom course. Day, evening, weekend and residential opportunities are available (indoor / outdoor rock climbing and archery also at this Centre, see "Day Camps"). Parts can be used towards Duke of Edinburgh Award Scheme. The centre is run by Bedfordshire County Council. 01234 854959. (See Advert page 14.)

Wyboston, Wyboston Lake. WS. 01480 213100.

B2 **Milton Keynes,** Milton Keynes Canoe Club, (BWB licence needed). C. 01234 713945. **The Caldecott Project.** C. S. W.

B2 01908 232042. **Willen Watersports & Activity Centre,** Willen Lake. C. S. W. 01908 670197.**Stewartby,** Stewartby Lake. S. WS. 01234 767751.

B3 **Rickmansworth,** Windsurfing and Canoeing Centre, Aquadrome, Frogmore La. (Jn 17, M25). Junior courses available in windsurfing and canoeing with qualified instructors allowing children to learn watersports in a relaxed, safe environment with the emphasis on fun. Beginners and improvers courses offered together with multi-activity days/weeks, a Kids Club and much more. 01923 771120. (See Advert below.)

C3 **Cheshunt,** Herts Young Mariners Base, Windmill La. C. K. S. W. Also Dragon boating. 01992 628403.

Lee Valley, Watersports Centre. S, W and WS on Banbury Lake. 0181 531 1129.

Stevenage, Fairlands Valley Lake. S. W. 01438 353241.

Welwyn Garden City, Stanborough Lakes. S. W.

ACTIVITIES

It's
Splashing Fun at

WATFORD SPRINGS
flumes and fast lanes

~ **Flumes** - two speeds - fast and faster!
~ **Beach Pool** - geysers, water jets and rapid ride
~ **Kiddies Harbour**
~ **Crèche facilities**

~ **Try Drop'n'Shop** - let the kids (8s and over) splash in the pool, while you splash out at the Harlequin centre.

Lower High Street, Watford, WD1 2NG (just off the ring road) For information call Watford Springs on 01923 211333

For safety reasons children under 8 years old must be accompanied by an adult at all times (maximum two children per adult)

TRIPS

Have a change from the car. Try the bus, the train, a boat or maybe a horse and cart!

TRIPS

BOAT TRIPS

Grand Union Canal. This canal, once the main waterway between London and Birmingham runs through Herts, Beds and Bucks and is navigable for much of its length. There are numerous things to do and see, opportunities to fish, or just watch the narrowboats negotiating the many flights of locks.

A3 **from Pitstone.** Trips from Pitstone Wharf. 01296 661920.

A4 **from Marlow.** Limited trips operate to Henley and Maidenhead during Summer school hols. 01865 243421.

B2 **from Leighton Buzzard.** Public trips along the Canal, *Easter, Bank Hols and some days in Aug.* 01525 384563.

Schools **from Milton Keynes.** Trips from Cosgrove Wharf, *weekends, Easter-Oct. weekdays during Summer School Hols.* 01604 862107.

B3 Schools **from Rickmansworth.** Batchworth Lock Centre, Church Street. Public boat trips and events are available between May and Sept, Suns only. Schools and groups on other days by arrangement. 01923 778382.

Schools **from Watford.** 75 min return canal trips, via two locks from Ironbridge Lock in Cassiobury Park. *Easter-Oct, Suns and Bank Hol Mons, at 2.30pm & 4pm and Tues & Thurs in Aug at 2.00 & 3.30pm.* 01438 714528.

C3 **River Lee.** A large stretch of the River Lee and part of the River Stort runs through East Hertfordshire before heading into Essex and London.

Schools **from Broxbourne,** Old Nazeing Road. Enjoy a cruise aboard an elegant, traditional style canal cruiser which offers a scheduled service every Summer Sunday *(Apr-Sept).* Special outings available and a range of boats for hire. 01992 462085.

Schools **from Sawbridgeworth.** Outings and children's excursions from the Maltings. 01279 600848.

BUS TRIPS

Leaside Travel are running over 800 day trips to lots of favourite places and with a Daytripper ticket, the prices are excellent value. Give the children a treat at Alton Towers, Legoland, Chessington World of Adventures or Thorpe Park. Prices are similar to the normal entry price, so with Daytripper you travel for free! Children of all ages love a day at the seaside, and there is a wide range of seaside trips going everywhere from Southend to Skegness, Walton on Naze to Weston Super Mare. But this is just a taster - there's much more to Daytripper. Daytrips run all around the country to many places of interest, and even to the continent. There is also a holiday programme where you can choose anything from Disneyland Paris to 5 days in Torquay, or even a 7 day tour of Ireland. There are many joining points in Herts and Essex, and local booking agents. More information: 0181 889 1184 or 01992 444444. (See Advert page 26.)

Map Ref: Please refer to map on page 4.
Price Codes for a family of four: **Ⓐ**: less than £5 **Ⓑ**: £5-£10 **Ⓒ**: £10-£15 **Ⓓ**: £15-20 **Ⓔ**: £20-£30 **Ⓖ**: Over £30 **Ⓕ**: Free
Schools: Range of educational opportunities available. 🎈 Birthday parties organised.

25

HORSE & CART RIDES

Penn. Horse and cart rides through the local area. 01494 817134.

Luton. Stockwood Country Park, offers carriage rides, adjacent to the Mossman Collection in the Stockwood Craft Museum. 01582 20766.

TRAIN TRIPS

©
Schools

Leighton Buzzard Railway, Billington Road, (A4146). Departing from Pages Park, this charming two-foot gauge railway chugs for five and a half miles past factories, houses and through the Bedfordshire countryside and back. Built in 1919 and originally used to serve local quarries, it now runs a regular passenger service through the Summer months. Several locomotives come from as far afield as India and West Africa. For 1997 there is a new cafe and indoor seating area and improved heritage/locomotive display areas. The souvenir shop and cafe are open at most times when trains are running. Special group rates are available including a popular "birthday break" package. Special events days are held throughout the year, including Teddy Bears' Outing. School's Specials operate by prior application. 01525 373888. Children 2-15 travel for £1 (See Advert page 23.)

LONDON

CONTENTS

Let's take a trip

Ⓖ
Open all year

↔
Victoria
Green Park
Marble Arch

The Big Bus Company. A visit to London is a magical moment in every child's life, one to be treasured forever. See London from the top of an open-top Big Bus. Your ticket is valid all day long with hop-on hop-off facility at over 31 central London locations allowing you the freedom to explore London at your leisure. Every tour has live commentary from friendly and most informative guides. Stopping points include the Tower of London, Big Ben, Madame Tussaud's, Harrods, Buckingham Palace and many more. Regular daily departures every 5-20 minutes throughout the year. It is an excellent service, well worth doing. For a brochure and further information contact The Big Bus Company, Waterside Way, London, SW17 7AB. 0181 944 7810. http://www.bigbus.co.uk. (See Advert page ii.)

Ⓒ / Ⓓ
Schools
Open all year

↔
Camden Town

Canal Waterbus will enable you to see a side of London that you never knew existed. Boat trips run along the historic Regents Canal between Camden Lock and picturesque Little Venice, with its island, wildfowl and boats. The trips pass through Regents Park, where you can get off to visit the Zoo, and the Maida Hill Tunnel and can include a stop for lunch, a picnic or shopping. Excellent educational resources and special group rates. *Trips run daily Apr-Oct, weekends only Nov-Mar.* Information: 0171 482 2660. Bookings: 0171 482 2550.

Ⓓ
Open all year

↔
Westminster
Tower Hill

Westminster - Tower Boat Trips. Discover London with the Red Fleet! Westminster to Tower or Tower to Westminster, whichever is your preference, a riverboat trip from Westminster Pier to the Tower of London, or vice versa is a **must** for any family visit to London. Excellent view of the Houses of Parliament, Big Ben, St. Paul's Cathedral, Tower of London and the magnificent Tower Bridge are combined with an interesting commentary on all of the sights given by a member of the crew. Whichever pier you start your cruise from you will find several other attractions you may wish to visit all within a short walking distance - many of them advertised in this publication. *Boat services commence at 10.20am from Apr-Oct running at 20 min intervals and from Nov-Mar from 10.30am every 45 mins. Services run until 9pm Jun-Aug. Closed Christmas Day.* 0171 930 8589. (See Advert page ii.)

Ⓔ / Ⓖ
↔
Westminster

Westminster - Kew & Hampton Court Boat Trips. Take a boat trip upriver from Westminster and combine a leisurely cruise with a visit to either Kew Gardens, Richmond or Hampton Court. Sit back and enjoy an interesting commentary about the historic sights including views of Big Ben, The Houses of Parliament, Lambeth Palace and some of the major London bridges. Further upstream you will pass through some of the prettier stretches of the Thames, and view country estates and houses from your vantage point on the river. *Regular sailings from Mar-Sept, with a limited service Oct.* 0171 930 2062/4721. (See Advert page iv.)

Ⓑ / Ⓒ
Open all year

↔
Tower Hill

Docklands Light Railway gives you easy access to London Docklands, one of the world's largest urban regeneration programmes which is transforming the former port area. Stunning modern architecture set amid historic docks, lots of activities, a Sunday Market, waterside shops and cafes are all worth seeing. Take the spectacular skyline ride on the Railway from Tower Gateway station, opposite the Tower of London with easy connection to the London Underground network. See Canary Wharf, go to the Visitor's Centre at Crossharbour or stop off at Mudchute to visit the Park and Farm. From the end of the line, Island Gardens, take the Victorian foot tunnel under the Thames to enjoy the delights of Greenwich. A Docklander ticket is good value giving you a day's unlimited travel to explore the area. Or, why not combine Docklands with Greenwich and a river boat trip with a "Sail & Rail" ticket available from Tower Gateway station or Westminster Pier. The ticket also gives you 20% off entry fee to the National Maritime Museum. 0171 363 9700 (24 hour answerphone). (See Advert page vi.)

LONDON

Price Codes for a family of four: Ⓐ: less than £5 Ⓑ: £5-£10 Ⓒ: £10-£15 Ⓓ: £15-£20 Ⓔ: £20-£30 Ⓖ:- Over £30 Ⓕ: Free
Schools: Range of educational opportunities available. 🕯 Birthday parties organised. ↔ Nearest tube station.

Let's Go to the Theatre

Ⓖ
Schools
Open all
year

↔
Victoria

Starlight Express, Apollo Victoria Theatre, is an exciting and spectacular production with stunning special effects and an amazing roller-coaster race track that encircles the auditorium and climbs high above the stalls to the dress circle, meeting on a hydraulically controlled bridge high above the stage area. The scene is set for action and the thrilling musical score races with the engines through a story of a battle for supremacy. The whole family will love it! An educational presentation and resource pack is available to school parties at excellent rates.   Enquiries to: The Really Useful Group, London WC2H 9NS. (See Advert page iv.)

Let's Visit

Ⓒ
Schools
Open all
year

↔
Tower Hill
London Bridge

HMS Belfast, off Morgans Lane, Tooley Street, is just a short walk from Tower Bridge. A real voyage of discovery awaits you here and will enthrall you and your children. HMS Belfast is the only surviving example of the great fleets of big gun armoured warships built for the Navy in the first half of this century. There is much to explore in the 187 metres of her length. You will encounter steep ladders and narrow passages when travelling from deck to deck and on the way you will see the sick bay and officers' cabins, the chapel, boiler and engine rooms, punishment rooms, the Admiral's bridge, the gun decks and more. Children will love the adventure here, but they must be supervised and care must be taken when using the ship's ladders. Not suitable for infants and disabled persons. Schools facilities: contact Sarah Hogben. *Open daily except Christmas period 24th-26th Dec, 10am-6pm (last admission 5.15pm), closes 5pm in Winter (last admission 4.15pm).* 0171 407 6434. (See Advert page iv.)

Ⓑ
Schools
Open all
year
◔

↔
Gunnersbury
Kew Gardens

Kew Bridge Steam Museum, Green Dragon Lane, **Brentford,** is located in a Victorian waterworks and houses a unique collection of steam pumping engines, the largest of which is over three storeys high! In Spring 1997 an exciting new permanent exhibition on water opens covering everything from potties to pipes right up to the new London Ring Main. There is also a childrens' activity centre! Engines are operated at weekends only or by arrangement for schools. A narrow gauge railway can be seen working with steam locomotive on selected weekends Mar-Nov. There is also a working waterwheel! School parties are welcome and offered practical educational opportunities. *Open daily (except Good Friday and Christmas) 11am-5pm, including Bank Hols.* 0181 568 4757 or send s.a.e. for 1997 events leaflet. (See Advert page xii.)

Ⓑ
Schools
Open all
year

↔
Gunnersbury

The London Aquatic Experience, Syon Park, **Brentford,** can be accessed from Brentford main line station, with a 15min. walk, or Kew Bridge station with a 237 or 267 bus ride. Here is a great day out for the family and a safe haven for many rescued and endangered species of unusual and beautiful fish, reptiles, amphibians, birds and small mammals. The animals are housed in self contained eco-systems to recreate their natural habitats. Find out why some fish simply hang motionless in the water, while others are constantly active. Learn about energy conservation from the reptiles and admire the inventiveness of many of the birds. There is much of interest here, lots to learn about the animals themselves and also about the important issues of conservation in the light of pollution, hunting and changing environments. There is a lecture theatre for school parties. *Open daily, except Christmas Day, 9am-6pm in Summer, 5pm in Winter.* 0181 847 4730. (See Advert page xii.)

Ⓓ
Schools
Open all
year

↔
Waterloo

Museum of the Moving Image is on the South Bank, close to Waterloo main line station or just a walk over the Hungerford footbridge from Embankment. This exciting and fascinating world of film, television and video will delight every member of the family. Explore the origin of film making, enjoy the glamour, discover some of the many secrets of film making and then have a go. There are opportunities to role play with actors on set; to read the news, to design your own cartoons and lots more opportunities to get involved! The museum is designed to reach children of all ages. Those under 3' tall have a new level from which to view the action and Sesame Street's Oscar the Grouch acts as a guide to help children identify the low-level exhibits. There is a good range of special exhibitions and Moving Magic Workshops frequently run in the school holidays where there are lots of drop-in activities organised for the family. Varied and interesting school party facilities. *Open daily except 24th-26th Dec, 10am-6pm (last admission 5pm).* 0171 401 2636. (See Advert page xiv.)

LONDON

Price Codes for a family of four: Ⓐ: less than £5   Ⓑ: £5-£10   Ⓒ: £10-£15   Ⓓ: £15-£20   Ⓔ: £20-£30   Ⓖ:- Over £30   Ⓕ: Free
Schools: Range of educational opportunities available.   ◕ Birthday parties organised.   ↔ Nearest tube station.

travel
through
time

Set out from Tower Bridge

Historic churches

Canary Wharf Tower

Lunch by the water

discover
Docklands and
Greenwich on
DLR

Start or finish your
journey on DLR by
riverboat from
Greenwich or
Westminster

Start your trip to Docklands and Greenwich on DLR from TOWER GATEWAY station - next to Tower Hill underground.
Or catch a boat from Westminster to Greenwich, crossing by foot tunnel under the Thames to pick up DLR at ISLAND GARDENS,
for a futuristic journey back through Docklands to central London.

i Leaflets available from Tourist Information Centres,
major hotels or ☎ 0171 363 9700.

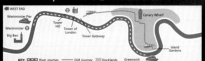

LGO

FREE VISITORS GUIDE

Past **PRESENT & FUTURE**

Take this voucher to Tower
Gateway or Island Gardens
Information Centre to recei
a free Visitors Guide!

DOCKLANDS
LIGHT RAIL

Let's Visit Pepsi Trocadero

Ⓕ **Pepsi Trocadero,** Piccadilly Circus, is not what it used to be. Having been redeveloped
Open all it is now Europe's largest entertainment complex. You will find virtual reality simulators, a
year multiplex cinema, exciting rides, themed restaurants, HMV and other shopping outlets, and
Segaworld, a brilliant futuractive indoor theme park (see below) as well as other exciting
attractions. You have fun everywhere, whether playing games, watching films, dining out or
↔ visiting the variety of attractions listed below. Pepsi Trocadero Information Line: 0990 100456.
Piccadilly (See Advert page ix.)
Circus

Ⓓ **The Emaginator:** Get strapped into four seater pods and try this revolutionary cinematic
experience! Not only will you see the film, you will experience it! There are 2 auditoria and 4
films are shown daily. *Open daily, 11am-10.15pm, closes 11pm Fri & Sat.* 0171 734 3271.

Ⓑ **Funland & Lazer Bowl:** High tech video game technology and latest craze bowling! *Open daily,
10am-1am.* 0171 287 8913.

Imax 3D Cinema: Opening Summer '97, a unique cinematic experience in a 302-seater
auditorium. The screen size, sound system, frame speed and 3D system will take your breath
away. Phone information line above for details.

Ⓓ **Madame Tussaud's Rock Circus:** See, feel and be moved by the true spirit of rock and pop
music with moving and static wax figures, archive film footage, memorabilia and personal
stereo sound surrounding you. You might be surprised who you bump into! *Open daily except
Christmas Day, 11am (except Tues, 12 noon)-9pm, (closes 10pm Fri & Sat).* 0171 734 7203.

Planet Hollywood: Dine in this film-themed restaurant which is full of memorabilia and other
surprises. *Open daily 11am-1am.*

Virgin Multiplex Cinema: with 7 screens. 0171 434 0031.

Ⓑ **Virtual Glider:** Hang glide through the "Grand Canyon" or over "Metropolis" - a challenging
VR experience for the fearless! *Open daily 10am-11pm.* 0171 287 8913.

Ⓓ **Virtual World:** Together with seven others, pilot your craft to exciting destinations and become
a "Sports Warrior" in Battletech, enter a war zone on Planet Solaris V11 and take control in this
first digital theme park! *Open daily 11am-11pm.* 0171 494 1992.

And including Segaworld!

Ⓖ **Segaworld,** a first in Europe, is a huge futuristic indoor theme park bringing a totally new
and innovative meaning to family entertainment. There are six major high-tech ride attractions
that are fully interactive and combine the excitement of motion simulation with virtual reality
imagery. You might start in Piccadilly, but you will fly into outer space or plumet to ocean
depths!

Hold on tight for six floors of interactive rides and experiences. The six futuristic themed zones
will thrill and chill: prepare to enter the world of Ghost Hunt and come face to face with demons
and ghouls; get to grips with 3D terrors of the deep in Aqua Planet; meet the challenge of Space
Mission, which will take you out of this world or calm your nerves with the magic of the
Carnival! After the rides visit the Interactive Games Zones. No visit here will ever be the same
twice; your experience will be unique every time! *Open daily, except Christmas Day, 10am-
midnight.* 0990 505040. (See Advert page viii.)

LONDON

Price Codes for a family of four: **Ⓐ**: less than £5 **Ⓑ**: £5-£10 **Ⓒ**: £10-£15 **Ⓓ**: £15-£20 **Ⓔ**: £20-£30 **Ⓖ**:- Over £30 **Ⓕ**: Free
Schools: Range of educational opportunities available. ● Birthday parties organised. ↔ Nearest tube station.

THE TROCADERO, PICCADILLY CIRCUS, LONDON

Experience the latest interactive entertainment
in the world's largest indoor theme park.

try telling your brain it's not real

© 1996 SEG

prepare your kids for the future

PEPSI TROCADERO ADRENALIN ZONE

Science fiction has just become reality.

Seven floors of sheer mind–blowing futuristic fun. Virtual reality, Segaworld, Planet Hollywood, cinemas, restaurants and shops now at the new Pepsi Trocadero, Piccadilly Circus, London.

For sensory overload, call for information on: **0990 100 456**

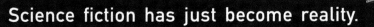

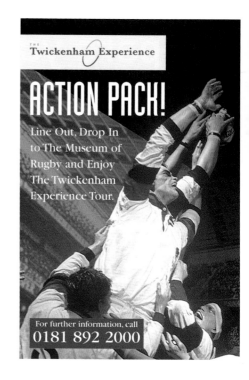

Ⓑ
Schools
Open all
year
💎

The Museum of Rugby and the Twickenham Experience Tours,
Rugby Road, **Twickenham,** a paradise for all enthusiasts, can be accessed by road, or by rail from Waterloo to Twickenham station. The home of English rugby has been impressively redeveloped and enlarged, incorporating the new and exciting multi-media Museum of Rugby. The history and growth of Rugby Union is charted using authentic mock-ups, interactive displays, archive film footage and unique objects. Also operating from the Museum are tours of the rugby stadium. You can walk alongside the hallowed turf, visit England's dressing room, walk through the players' tunnel and enjoy the magnificent views of the entire stadium from the top of the North Stand. *Open non-match days: Tues-Sat & Bank Hols 10.30am-5pm, Sun, 2-5pm. Match days: open for match ticket holders only 11am-1 hour before kick-off. Closed 25th-26th Dec and Good Fri.* 0181 892 2000. (See Advert page x.)

Ⓓ
Schools
Open all
year

↔
South
Kensington

The Natural History Museum, Cromwell Road, sited in a most magnificent building, houses an amazing world of natural treasures and provides an opportunity to explore the Earth and its life, both past and present under one roof. See real dinosaur skeletons and life-size robotic dinosaur models in 'Dinosaurs'. Marvel at the miracle of life in 'Human Biology' and walk under an erupting volcano and experience an earthquake in 'The power within'. To get the most out of your visit, focus on one or two of the fascinating exhibitions and return another day for more! (Find out about the excellent membership offers.) *Open daily, except 23rd-26th Dec, Mon-Sat 10am-5.50pm, Sun 11am-5.50pm.* 0171 938 9123. (See Advert page x.)

Ⓒ
Schools
Open all
year

↔
Tower Hill

The Tower Bridge Experience, Tower Bridge, is close to Tower Hill underground and London Bridge station and accessible by river boat and bus. Journey back through time as you step into the heart of The Tower Bridge Experience, situated inside London's famous landmark. Here, exciting animatronics and interactive displays bring to life more than 100 years of the bridge's amazing history. You'll discover London in the 1890s, why the bridge was built and how it works and you'll never forget the spectacular views of the London skyline and the River Thames, from the high-level walkways. You can also visit the magnificent Victorian steam engine rooms to experiment with hands-on working models. Self guided tours take about 90 minutes. There are excellent educational facilities. *Open daily except 24th-26th Dec, & 1st Jan; also closed for maintenance, 4th Wed in Jan. Nov-Mar: 9.30am-6pm. Apr-Oct: 10am-6.30pm.* 0171 378 1928. (See Advert page x.)

Ⓔ
Schools
Open all
year

↔
Tower Hill

The Tower of London is one of the world's most famous fortified buildings. In its 900 year history, it has been a fortress, prison, the Royal Mint and even a zoo! A day out at the Tower of London brings the past to life, as free Yeoman Warder tours lead the visitor on a dramatic journey through its fascinating and often gory history from 1078 through to the present day. *Open 1st Mar-31st Oct. Mon-Sat, 9am-6pm, Sun, 10am-6pm. From 1st Nov-28th Feb, Tues-Sat, 9am-5pm, Sun & Mon, 10am-5pm. Closed 24th-26th Dec & 1st Jan. Last admission 1 hour before closing.* 0171 709 0765.

Ⓓ
Schools
Open all
year

↔
Wembley
Park

Wembley Stadium Tours. This is a unique opportunity to see behind the scenes at this famous stadium and is certain to thrill children of most ages! The tour, conducted by Desmond Lynam on laser disc, lasts about one and a half hours and takes you to areas not normally available to the public. See The Event Control Rooms, the nerve centre of the major event day operations and visit the Television Studios. Re-live Wembley's Greatest Moments in a special cinema presentation and then join the Wembley Land Train to enjoy an educational fun ride with full commentary highlighting events from Wembley's history. Visit England Changing Rooms, walk up to the Players' Tunnel and climb up the famous 39 steps as if to receive the Wembley Cup. Look out for the new 1966 World Cup gallery. *Open Apr-Sept, 10am-4pm, Oct-Mar, 10am-3pm. Tour operates daily except 25th, 26th Dec and Event Days.* Please call to check in advance. 0181 902 8833. (See Advert page x.)

LONDON

Price Codes for a family of four: Ⓐ: less than £5   Ⓑ: £5-£10   Ⓒ: £10-£15   Ⓓ: £15-£20   Ⓔ: £20-£30   Ⓖ: Over £30   Ⓕ: Free
Schools: Range of educational opportunities available.   💎 Birthday parties organised.   ↔ Nearest tube station.

xi

Ⓕ **Parks:** St. James', Green Park, Hyde Park and Regent's Park are all excellent for relief from the city streets. Feed the ducks or picnic in the Summer.

Ⓕ
↔
St. Pauls
St. Paul's Cathedral is splendid and awe-inspiring. A great feat of architecture and much fun climbing up to the various galleries for great views. (Charge for galleries.)

Ⓕ **Westminster** must be seen with the Houses of Parliament, Big Ben and Westminster Abbey to admire. There is a lovely view of the House of Commons and the House of Lords from Westminster Bridge. Monarchs are crowned in the Abbey and many famous people are buried there. See how many you can find. Take a look in Parliament Square to see how many Prime

↔
Westminster
Ministers have a statue there. Just a short walk away up Whitehall is the entrance to Downing Street. Who lives at No. 10?

Ⓑ
Schools
Open all year
Wimbledon Lawn Tennis Museum, Church Road, 15 mins walk from the underground, or 25 mins walk from the mainline station, tells the story of lawn tennis and how the game began. Displays range from a Victorian Parlour to a Racket Maker's Workshop and the collections include costumes, paintings, ornaments and jewellery all illustrating the tennis theme. Look out over Centre Court, see videos of great champions in the audio visual theatre or try an animated quiz to test your knowledge of Wimbledon. A visit here is a must for all enthusiasts, but you don't have to be a tennis lover to appreciate this lovely museum, there is such a lot to enjoy. *Open Tues-Sat, & Bank Hol Mons (in Summer), 10.30am-5pm, Suns, 2-5pm. Closed Fri, Sat, Sun prior*

↔
Wimbledon
to Championships and middle Sunday of same. During the Wimbledon fortnight, admission is for ticket holders only. 0181 946 6131. (See Advert page xii.)

Ⓒ
Open all year
The London Toy & Model Museum, 21/23 Craven Hill. See, hear and touch interactive exhibits in themed galleries ranging from a Victorian Nursery to a First World War trench, the deck of a steam ship and a Teddy Bears' Picnic deep in the woods. Relax in the Museum's landscaped walled garden where activities include a children's carousel and ride-on

↔
Paddington
trains. *Open daily, 9am-5.30pm. Last admission 4.30pm. (Thurs 9pm). (Sun and Bank Hols 11am-5.30pm.)* 0171 402 5222.

LONDON

WIN TICKETS TO THE ATTRACTIONS

£500 WORTH OF ENTRANCE TICKETS TO BE WON!

All you have to do is answer the questions opposite. Fill in your name and address on the reverse side and send it to the address overleaf before 30th September 1997.

LONDON COMPETITION

1. Which River flows through London?

2. Which is the only lifting bridge in London?

3. Where does the Prime Minister live?

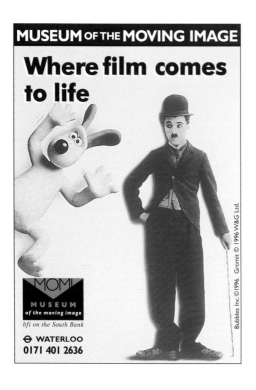

Competition Reply Slip

Name...

Address..

....

....

Age...

What is your favourite London attraction?

....

Have you bought a Let's Go with the Children edition before?

YES☐   NO☐

COMPETITION

Make sure your entries reach us by 30th September 1997.
The winners will be the first correct entries drawn. Winners will be notified by post during October 1997.
No responsibility can be accepted for entries lost, defaced or delayed in the post. No correspondence can be entered into and the decision of the publishing company is final.

Send the reply slip to:
London Competition
Cube Publications,
Bank House, Mavins Road,
Farnham,
Surrey GU9 8JS

Ⓕ **Trafalgar Square** is always fun. Nelson commands the Square, the lions stand guard while
↔ the fountains play. Sit awhile on the steps and enjoy a break here but be warned you will have to
Charing Cross share your sandwich with the pigeons!

Let's Play

Ⓑ **big fish,** 78a Frith Road, **Croydon,** is a fun indoor play centre for up to 11 year olds which has
Open all been recently redecorated under new ownership. Ball pools, a rope bridge and roller presses add
year to the excitement here. Children can play in the Spooky House which has its own ghost and
toddlers have a separate soft play area with their own telephone kiosk. Holiday activities, special
Hallowe'en and Christmas parties, and excellent birthday parties are organised. The cafe, where
parents can watch and wait, has television. *Open daily, 10am-6pm.* 0181 781 1661. (See Advert page
xiv.)

Ⓐ per child **Snakes and Ladders,** Syon Park, **Brentford,** is well signposted from Syon Park or can be
Open all accessed via 237 or 267 bus from Kew Bridge BR or Gunnersbury Underground station. Children
year can find action packed fun whatever the weather. They can let off steam in the giant supervised
indoor main playframe, intermediate 2-5s area or toddlers area or use the outdoor adventure
playground when the sun shines. A mini motor bike circuit provides an exciting additional
↔ activity. Meanwhile parents can relax in the cafe overlooking the playframe. *Open daily 10am-6pm.*
Gunnersbury *Last admission 5.15pm.* All children must wear socks. 0181 847 0946.

Let's Eat

The Chicago Pizza Pie Factory, 17 Hanover Square. Take the family to Chicago and
let the Pizza Pie Factory give you all a real treat! Every Sunday from 12 noon-4.30pm, there is fun
and adventure here for all the family with free games and entertainment for children aged 3-10
years. The Funday is hosted by the resident balloon twisting clown "Smarty Arty" with story-
tellers and face painters to ensure a party atmosphere. The activities take place in the fully
↔ supervised "boardroom" away from the restaurant, so parents can enjoy a meal in peace! Call 0171
Oxford Circus 629 2552 for reservations. (See Advert page below.)

LONDON

xv

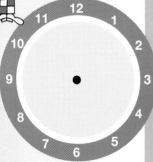
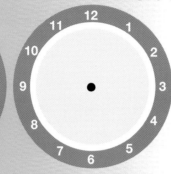

FUN PARKS

A wide variety of entertainment laid on. Great ideas for a treat!

A3
Ⓑ
Open all year
🔍

Fit for Kids, Beech Rd., off London Rd., **High Wycombe,** is an indoor play area for children up to 12 years with a separate area for under 4s. *Open daily, Tues-Sun, 10am-6.30pm, Suns, 10am-5.30pm. Open Mons, Bank Hols & School Hols.* 01494 538115.

Ⓑ
Open all year
🔍

Kid Zone, Gatehouse Close, **Aylesbury.** A large indoor play area with a dedicated area for under 5s. Try the giant jelly mountain or the car wash rollers. *Open daily, 9.30am-7pm, School Summer Hols, 9.30am-6pm.* Height limit, 5ft. max. 01296 330405.

Ⓑ
Open all year
🔍

Moonbase at the Wycombe Sports Centre, Marlow Hill is an Indoor Adventure Play area. Try the vertical roller squeeze. There is a separate Toddlers area. *Open daily, Mon-Fri 10am-6pm, Sat & Sun 10am-5pm.* 01494 446324.

B2
Ⓑ
Open all year
🔍

Activity World, Rollers, The Denbigh Centre, Saxon St., **Milton Keynes** (V7). An exciting indoor playground for those under 4' 9". Slides, ball ponds, ropes, nets, mazes and a Hamster wheel. *Open daily, 9.30am-7.30pm.* 01733 558774.

Ⓔ
Open all year

Woburn Safari Park, Jn 13 off the M1. The Leisure Park includes a boating lake and a superb indoor activity playground for 6-15 year olds. Entrance here is combined with the drive through Safari Park. 01525 290407. (See "Discover" for Abbey and "Nature" chapters and Advert page 46.)

B3
Ⓑ
Open all year
🔍

Adventure World, Perham Way, **London Colney.** Climb the monster mountain and challenge the death slide and crocodile ravine. For under 5s, there is a separate indoor soft play area. *Open Mon & Fri, 10am-7pm, Sat, Sun, 9am-7pm; Tues-Thurs & Bank Hols, 10am-6pm.* 01727 822447.

Ⓑ
Open all year
🔍

Jungle Gym, Amazone, Gade House, 46 The Parade, **Watford.** Two indoor play areas, one for tiny tots and one for 6-12 year olds on the Amazone jungle trail. *Open daily, 10am-11pm (last session starts at 7pm).* 01923 222223.

🔍 Ⓑ
Open all year

Kidspace, Greatham Rd. Ind. Estate, off Water Lane, **Watford.** Plunge through the Black Hole or climb the giant inflatable Martian Mountain at this new 'place in space' for 2-14 year olds. *Open daily, 9.30am-7.30pm.* 01923 223235.

🔍 Ⓑ
Open all year

Kid Zone, Northbridge Road, **Berkhamsted.** Here is the place to play where the weather can't stop the fun! Dare the Death Drop Slide, the viewing walkways and the supersonic gliders. Toddlers' soft play area. *Open daily, 9.30am-7pm.* 01442 878441.

Ⓐ / Ⓑ
Schools
Open all year

Play Dome, Woodside Leisure Park, Garston, **Watford.** Play Dome is a huge, new, indoor Adventure Playground operated by the David Lloyd Leisure organisation, offering fun-filled action for children up to 12 years. Built on three storeys, the main play area has an exciting 4 metre free-fall slide and twisting tube slides, net crawls, bridges, aerial runways, rope swings and much more. There is a separate under 5s section with soft play area and an Activities room full of painting, Duplo and other play equipment. This is the first PlayDome site in Britain. *Open daily, Mon-Fri 9.30am-6pm, Sat, Sun & School hols, 10am-7pm.* 01923 894801. (See Advert page 44.)

Ⓑ
Open all year
🔍

The Playground, Blackburn Rd, **Houghton Regis.** An indoor adventure playground with a play village for the under 7s and another for under 3s. Trampolining available for under 14s. *Open daily, 9am-7pm.* 01582 660111.

Ⓑ
Schools
🔍

Safari Adventure, Lincolnsfields Centre, Bushey Hall Drive (off Aldenham Rd), **Bushey.** Non-stop bouncing fun in this indoor soft playworld for children up to 12 years. *Open Tues-Sun, 10.30am-5.15pm from Easter-end Oct, then weekends & School hols in Winter.* 01923 233841. (See also "Nature" chapter and Advert page 45.)

Map Ref: Please refer to map on page 4.

Price Codes for a family of four: **Ⓐ:** less than £5 **Ⓑ:** £5-£10 **Ⓒ:** £10-£15 **Ⓓ:** £15-£20 **Ⓔ:** £20-£30 **Ⓖ:** Over £30 **Ⓕ:** Free

Schools: Range of educational opportunities available. 🔍 Birthday parties organised.

43

FUN PARKS

FORT KNEBWORTH

EXCITING ADVENTURE PLAYGROUND

CHILDREN LOVE IT!

Daily: 22 March - 7 April; 24 May -2 Sept. Weekends &
Bank Hols from12th April- 18th May; weekends only
from 6 Sept-28 Sept. House open as above except
closed Mondays. Open Bank Holiday Mondays.
ENTRANCE DIRECT FROM JUNCTION 7 OF THE
A1(M) AT STEVENAGE. TEL. 01438-812661

KNEBWORTH
STEVENAGE
HERTS

Bring this advertisement for 50p off
Child entrance ticket when
accompanied by one
full paying
adult.

SWIM SCHOOL
THE BEST WAY TO LEARN

★ Extensive programme

★ Any age, any ability

★ Private lessons available

★ Exclusive awards scheme

★ Stroke technique has priority

★ Above all a fun environment

Dunstable Leisure Centre
Court Drive, Dunstable, Bedfordshire
Telephone: (01582) 608107
Dunstable Leisure Centre is managed by Circa Leisure
plc on behalf of South Bedfordshire District Council

Watford

**Woodside Leisure Park,
Kingsway, Garston,
Watford,**

**General Enquiries:
01923 894 801**

**Party Bookings:
01923 894 802**

◉ 4 Metre Free Fall Slide
◉ Twisting Tube Slides
◉ Ramps ◉ Net Crawls
◉ Bridges ◉ Aerial Runways
◉ Tunnels ◉ Ball Pools
◉ Rope Swings
and lots more!

Children's Party Package available!

Fully Supervised Indoor Adventure Playground

PlayDome is a massive, fun filled, supervised playground, providing an exciting, yet safe
environment where children up to the age of 12 can become physically fit whilst having lots of fun!

**Separate under 5's Play Frame and Activity Room, with Play Dough,
Painting, Puzzles, Duplo, Push along Toys and Much more!**

Admission Prices for 1 1/2 Hours of Play
● Under 5's £3.25 ● Parents & Babies in arm FREE ● Over 5's
£4.25 ● Mother & Toddler sessions £2.75 ● Gold Members 50p off
each session ● Discounts for Group Bookings, Schools and Clubs

Opening Hours
◉ Weekdays 9.30am - 6.30pm
◉ Weekends & School Holidays
10am - 7pm

B4 Ⓑ Open all year Ⓠ

Zoom, Station Rd., **Beaconsfield,** offers loads of fun for children from 2-12 years even when the weather is wet. Large playframe with slides, ball ponds and soft play. *Open daily, 10am-6pm weekdays & Suns, 9am-6pm Sats.* 01494 673005.

C3 Ⓑ Open all year Ⓠ

Activity World, Longmead, Birchwood, **Hatfield.** Enter a world of Dizzy Donuts, Ballpools, mirrors, swings and much more for children under 5'. Toddler areas. *Open daily, 9.30am-7.30pm.* 01733 558774.

Ⓐ Open all year Ⓠ

Adventure Island Playbarn, Parsonage Lane, **Sawbridgeworth.** This indoor softplay centre has lots of features including a ball pond and aerial runway. There is a separate area for toddlers. The outdoor picnic area has a bouncy castle and play equipment. Height restriction 4'9". *Open 10am-6pm.* 01279 600907.

Ⓑ Open all year Ⓠ

Carter's Crazy House, Stevenage. Conquer the skywalk nets and race the astra slides in this indoor adventure playground in the town centre. The Playground is supervised at all times. *Open daily, 10am-6pm.* 01438 747983.

Ⓒ Schools

Knebworth Park and Playground. Children love 'Fort Knebworth', a super wooden adventure fortress with a huge Astroglide, space tubes, bouncy castle, monorail suspension slide, skate board 'bowl', Tarzan Trail, plus extra thrills on the new Corkscrew and Freefall slides. There is a separate miniature railway. *Park open daily 22nd Mar-7th Apr, 24th May-2nd Sept. Weekends and Bank Hols only 12th Apr-18th May and weekends only 6th-28th Sept. 11am-5.30pm.* 01438 812661. (See Advert page 44.)

Ⓑ Open all year

Toddler World, Galleria, **Hatfield.** Children up to 4' can revel in the playshapes, tower climb, ball pond, slides, maze, tunnel, log cabin and much more. *Open daily, Mon-Sat, 10am-6pm, Sun, 11am-5pm.* 01707 257480.

46

NATURE

All children love animals and there are many to see here from cuddly farm favourites to more unusual species!

MAP REFS **PRICE CODES**

A3

Schools
Open all year
Ⓑ
Q

The Bucks Goat Centre, Layby Farm, Old Risborough Road, **Stoke Mandeville,** just off the A4010 on the southern side of the village. This is a rare example of an open farm and a marvellous place to take the youngest of children. Examples of all the breeds of goat kept in Britain can be seen at close quarters and bags of feed for them can be purchased. On a short, safe farm walk, sheep, poultry, rabbits and other small farm livestock can be seen together with an educational display of information about the stock. Conducted tours are available for school parties and donkey rides are available most weekends. There is a children's play area, several shops, a cafe and a plant nursery. Goat produce is on sale in the Farm Shop. *Open Tues-Sun, 10am-5pm, also Bank Hols.* 01296 612983. (See Advert page 63.)

Q Ⓑ
Schools
Open all year

Gibbons Farm Rare Breeds Centre, Horsleys Green, **Stokenchurch,** signposted off B482, is a traditional farm with pigs, cattle, sheep and other small animals. Special event days. Teashop in renovated barn open daily. *Open daily, 10am-6pm.* 01494 482385.

Ⓕ
Open all year

Home of Rest for Horses, Princes Risborough. See "Fun for Free" chapter and Advert page 11.

Ⓑ
Schools
Q

Oak Farm Rare Breeds Park, Broughton, **Aylesbury,** is on the eastern edge of Aylesbury, off A41, signed to Broughton. There is a wide variety of animals to see and they all have names. Unusual poultry show off their chicks, rare sheep of all sizes roam with their lambs and a real Aylesbury duck may stage an appearance on the pond. In the barns, the animals can be seen at close quarters. Read Matilda the Goat's "Fussy Farm Facts" and try the farm quiz. There is also an exhibition centre, play area, countryside walk and "Nigel the Know-all Newt's Nature Trail". Picnic inside or out. Special food is available for hand feeding the animals. Highly recommended. *Open, Easter-end Aug, Sat & Sun, Wed, Thur, Fri & Bank Hols, 10.30am-5.30pm. Sept & Oct Sat & Sun only.* 01296 415709. (See Advert page 46.)

B2

Schools
Open all year
Ⓐ

Emberton Country Park, on the A509, covers 195 acres and includes 40 acres of lakes, used for fishing and sailing. There is a pitch & putt course, orienteering course, nature trail and two play areas. *Open daily.* 01234 711575.

Ⓑ
Schools
Q

Mead Open Farm, is situated just outside Leighton Buzzard in the village of **Billington,** signed from the A505 and A4146. There is a relaxed atmosphere in this family run farm with lots of space for children in a safe environment. Apart from the usual farm animals there are a number of rare breeds to see. Rabbit handling, lamb bottle-feeding and goat milking are all held throughout the season in the indoor pets corner which also houses well displayed educational material. There is a tea room and gift shop and the children will love the outside play area with the ride-on pedal tractor circuit and log play area. There are special weekend events such as magic days, sheep dog demonstrations and traditional harvesting/threshing days. *Open Tues-Sun, mid Mar-end Oct, 10am-5pm.* 01525 852954. (See Advert page 46.)

Ⓑ

Toddington Manor, is five minutes from the M1 (Jn 12). This country estate is divided into three areas; the old piggery, where some of the rare breeds of livestock and the vintage tractors can be seen; the gardens and the lakes and woods. Children can borrow nets and buckets and try pond dipping. *Open May-Sept, Wed-Sun, 11am-6pm.* 01525 873924/872576.

Q Ⓔ
Schools
Open all year

Woburn Safari Park, on the A4012, 5 minutes from M1, Jn. 13, is an exciting Safari Park providing fun-filled family adventure. Experience the excitement of being only a windscreen's width away from enormous elephants, hippos, giraffes, lions, zebras, mischievous monkeys and more. After a drive through the spectacular 300

NATURE

Map Ref: Please refer to map on page 4.
Price Codes for a family of four: Ⓐ: less than £5 Ⓑ: £5-£10 Ⓒ: £10-£15 Ⓓ: £15-£20 Ⓔ: £20-£30 Ⓖ:- Over £30 Ⓕ: Free
Schools: Range of educational opportunities available. Q Birthday parties organised.

Family Fun!
on a Working Farm

Visit Bowmans Open Farm for that special day out for all the family.

Whether you are enjoying a School Holiday or looking for a relaxing day away from the hustle & bustle - Bowmans Open Farm has something for everyone!

• Enjoy a relaxing stroll along the **Farm Trail** & see modern farming at work

• Meet the **Farm Characters: Ben** the Shire Horse, **William** the enormous Friesian Bull & look out for Spritzer the friendly Farmer's Dog.

•Meander through **Pets Corner** amongst the **Rabbits, Chickens, Ducks** & **Guinea Pigs.** Can you spot the **Non Water-Proofed Duck.**

• Climb on the **Old Tractor** or try a **Tractor Ride!**
• Come & have fun in our **Adventure Playground** or **Teeny Tots Adventure Playground!**

• See The Feather Perfect Falconry display team. View our selection of hawks, falcons, owls and eagles at close quarters and marvel at the breathtaking free flying displays.

• Browse in the **Farm Shop!** There's a wonderful selection to choose from; award-winning butchery counter, delicious pickles & preserves, mouth-watering pastries & pies. Plus our own Farm-made Bowmans Premier Dairy Product Range!

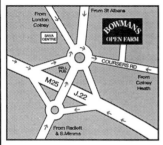

• Relax in the **Restaurant** or on the patio with Cakes & Pastries galore! Open for Morning Coffee, Lunch & Afternoon Tea! Why not book your children's party or business function in the Banqueting Suite!

• Find Us just off M25 J.22

TELEPHONE:
01727 822106

Open Every Day 9am - 5.30pm

Bowmans Open Farm, Coursers Road, London Colney, Herts AL2 1BB

ESTABLISHED 1932
~BOWMANS~
OPEN FARM

acre Safari Park, the younger ones can feed the pygmy goats in Pets' Corner or run wild in the Adventure Ark on rope ladders and astra slides. Interact with iguanas, or communicate with camels in the fascinating Wildwatch Computer Centre. For the fourth consecutive year there are more new attractions at Woburn, including the new Tree Top Action Trail. A fantastic place for a great, all-inclusive family day out in a beautiful and historic setting. *Open daily, Mar-Oct, 10am-5pm (last admission), Nov-Feb, weekends only, 11am-3pm (last admission).* 01525 290407. (See Advert page 46 also "Discover" and "Fun Parks" chapters.)

B3 ⓑ **Binghams Park Farm,** Potten End Hill, Water End, **Hemel Hempstead**. This
Schools newly opened farm is keen to retain old countryside traditions. Children are
Open all year encouraged to touch, hold and feed the friendly farm animals, many of which are rare
🎈 breeds. There are Scarecrow trails and treasure hunts through the woods, tractor and trailer rides and activity weekends, reviving old crafts and festivals. Special toddler and children's parties, along with educational tours for all levels, can be arranged. With an excellent farm shop and small cafe, outdoor picnic area and seasonal Pick Your Own there is fun for all age groups. *Open daily, 9am-5.30pm. Children's farm closes at dusk in the Winter.* 01442 232373. (See Advert page 50.)

ⓒ **Bowmans Farm,** Coursers Road, **London Colney,** just off the M25 at Jn 22 and
Schools close to St. Albans, offers an enjoyable and active day out for the whole family. The
Open all year working farm has a variety of animals for you to meet, including William the Bull and
🎈 Ben the Shire Horse. Admire the young piglets, calves and lambs in their natural environment, and join the rabbits, ducks and guinea pigs in the huge Pets' Corner. Make sure you visit the impressive new Falconry Centre, where you can see falcons, owls and hawks flying daily. You can also get a bird's eye view of cows being milked in the parlour from a special viewing Gallery. There is much more to enjoy around the farm, including lakeside walks, tractor rides, picnic area and an exciting adventure playground, which provides a great opportunity for children to let off steam. Stop off at the restaurant, where you can try Bowmans ice cream made on the farm, and browse around the farm, craft and country shops. Lots of excellent education information around to add interest to your visit. *Open daily, 9am-5.30pm (5pm Winter).* 01727 822106. (See Advert page 48.)

ⓑ **Chalfont Shire Horse Centre,** Gorelands La, **Chalfont St. Giles,** signed
Schools from the A413. Gentle giants to see and demonstrations are held when the
🎈 magnificent heavy horses are put through their paces. There is also a play area and blacksmith's shop. *Open Mar-Sept, Sat, Sun & Bank Hols. and daily in School hols, 10am-4.30pm.* 01494 872304.

ⓐ **College Lake Wildlife Centre,** Tring, is on the B488 at Bulbourne and is
Schools a BBONT Nature Reserve and working farm museum. It has marshes, woodland and
Open all year lakes. Bee, butterfly and wildlife gardening centres have recently been opened. *Open daily, 10am-5pm.* 01296 668805.

ⓕ Schools **Herts & Middlesex Wildlife Trust,** St. Albans. See "Fun for Free"
Open all year chapter.

ⓐ **Langleybury School Farm,** Langleybury La, **Hunton Bridge.** Many
Schools domestic farm animals to see in this open farm run by the neighbouring school's PTA.
🎈 Group visits by prior arrangement. Enjoy also the aviary and deer, pony rides and special fun days. *Open Easter-Oct, Sat, Sun, Bank Hol Mons, 11am-4pm. Summer School hols, 12-4pm.* 01923 270603.

B3 ⓐ **Lincolnsfields Centre,** Bushey Hall Drive, **Bushey.** The animal encounter
Schools section of this centre lets children get really close to rare breeds of farm animals and
Open all year domestic pets. Rabbits run free - there is a turtle pond and you can stroke the guinea
🎈 pigs and meet 'Hooty' the barn owl and 'Kissie' the buzzard. New for 1997 is a "Bug House". *Open daily, Mon, 1-5pm, Tues-Sun, 10am-5pm.* 01923 233841. (See also "Fun Parks" chapter and Advert page 45.)

NATURE

Map Ref: Please refer to map on page 4.
Price Codes for a family of four: ⓐ: less than £5 ⓑ: £5-£10 ⓒ: £10-£15 ⓓ: £15-£20 ⓔ: £20-£30 ⓖ:- Over £30 ⓕ: Free
Schools: Range of educational opportunities available. 🎈 Birthday parties organised.

49

B3 Ⓑ Schools Open all year

Longford Childrens Farm, Great Gaddesden, near Hemel Hempstead

just off the A4146, has a farm trail and there are many animals to enjoy at close hand. You have the chance to meet Rosie the Shetland pony, Jonjo and Oliver, the friendly goats, Emily and Muffin, the donkeys, along with a variety of sheep, pigs, ducks, chickens and rabbits. If you are lucky Oliver, the friendly goat, might escort you round. Grain and seed are available at a small charge to feed the animals. There is a coffee shop, a farm shop and many species of animals are bred for sale. *Open daily, 9am-5pm.* 01442 843471. (See Advert page 50.)

Ⓔ Schools Open all year

Whipsnade Wild Animal Park, Dunstable, was the world's first open-

planned zoo and is set in 600 acres of open parkland, signed from M1 and A5. It is home to over 2,500 animals including elephants, penguins, bears, tigers and giraffes. Leave time in your day for a trip on the narrow gauge railway and look out for the Children's Farm and Discovery Centre. *Open daily, except Christmas Day, 10am-6pm (4pm in Winter).* 01582 872171.

Ⓑ Schools Open all year Ⓠ

Woodside Farm & Wild Fowl Park, Luton, one of Britain's largest

Poultry Centres, is situated on the outskirts of the village on the B4540, just 2 miles from the M1, Jn9 coming from the South, or 2 miles from the M1, Jn10 coming from the North. (Follow the brown tourist signs.) There are over 160 different breeds of animals and birds to see and feed with the special rations from the Farm Shop. The waterfowl parks, pheasantry, 'Animals at Home' and the piggery, all house many rare and pure breeds. Large areas for picnics, indoors and outdoors, with pony rides, tarzan trails, forts, nurserylands, farm tractors, bouncy castles, birds of prey, and tractor and trailer rides round the Park daily. There is entertainment in the Park, during the year, with special celebrations in December, when Father Christmas visits! Also visit the large indoor Rabbit and Guinea Pig Warren, pets corner, where all the children and adults can stroke and handle the animals, and can collect fresh eggs straight from the Hen House. Under 5s Mini Tractor Play Area and new enlarged owl display. *Open daily, except Suns, Christmas and New Year's Day, 8am-5.30pm.* 01582 841044. (See Advert page 50.)

B4 Ⓒ Schools Open all year Ⓠ

Odds Farm Park - Rare Breeds Centre, Wooburn Common, Nr.

Beaconsfield. Within easy reach of the M4 and M40, this Farm Park is one of a select group to receive "Approval" from the Rare Breeds Survival Trust. Information on each of the breeds is clearly displayed. A pets corner allows children to get to know smaller breeds, such as rabbits and guinea pigs. Facilities include: tea room, gift shop, log play area with a separate area for under 5s, toilet facilities, mother & baby room and ample parking. Daily "Hands-On" activity programme, including bottle feeding lambs, goat milking, calf and chicken feeding, collecting eggs or "Pat a Pet" if wet. Tractor and trailer rides and indoor playbarn, some activities are seasonal. Weekend events throughout the year. *Open daily, Apr-mid Sept, 10am-5pm; mid Sept-Mar, Thurs-Sun, 10am-4pm. Open all school hols.* 01628 520188. (See Advert page 45).

C2 Ⓑ Open all year

The Royal Society for the Protection of Birds, The Lodge,

Sandy on B1042. 106 acres of woodland surround a 19th century house. Though principally a bird reserve, other wildlife including grey squirrels and muntjak deer can be seen along the nature trail. *Reserve open daily, 9am-9pm or dusk.* 01767 680541. Ⓕ to RSPB and YOC members.

Ⓑ Schools

Standalone Farm, Wilbury Rd, Letchworth Garden City. Standalone is one

of the best examples of a working open farm in Herts with cattle, sheep, pigs and poultry and many of the other traditional farmyard animals including goats, ducks, geese, donkeys and two magnificent Shire Horses, Sam and Webster. Visit during the springtime and see the newborn lambs. Watch the daily milking demonstration, follow the nature trail to the hides at the Wildfowl area and enjoy displays in the Exhibition Barn. Bring your own picnic and take advantage of the indoor and outdoor picnic areas, or buy refreshments from the shop which also sells fresh eggs and souvenirs. Schools and playgroups welcome by prior arrangement and teachers

NATURE

Map Ref: Please refer to map on page 4.
Price Codes for a family of four: Ⓐ: less than £5 Ⓑ: £5-£10 Ⓒ: £10-£15 Ⓓ: £15-£20 Ⓔ: £20-£30 Ⓖ:- Over £30 Ⓕ: Free
Schools: Range of educational opportunities available. ● Birthday parties organised.

51

STANDALONE FARM

A warm welcome awaits you

Open everyday 11am to 5pm (inc Bank Holidays). From March to September inclusive and Herts Autumn Half Term week. Indoor and outdoor picnic areas, refreshments available. Groups welcome by arrangement.

Tel: 01462 686775 Wilbury Road, Letchworth Garden City

 LETCHWORTH GARDEN CITY

Standalone Farm is a Letchworth Garden City Heritage Foundation Enterprise

FAMILY SEASON TICKETS £26.00

Our daily activities include... New for 1997 - 'Dr. Do & Dr. Little's Desert Island Adventure • Wild West Parrot Show • Mr & Mrs Noah's Fun Boat (indoor play area) • Pirates Cove Play Area - Plus, meet the birds of prey and our tiger and lion cubs.

As well as the superb animal park there are a whole host of other attractions at Paradise Wildlife Park, including, The Woodland Railway, Adventureland, Fantasyland, Crazy Golf, pony rides and a souvenir shop to name but a few! On site snacks and refreshments are available from a range of outlets.

Admission Prices

Adults **£5.00**
Senior Citizens **£4.00**
Children (2-15) **£4.00**

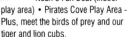

Where the animals come to meet you!

Find Us At...

White Stubbs Lane, Broxbourne, Hertfordshire. **01992 468001**

seminars and educational material is available. A Family Season Ticket enables you to visit as many times as you like during the season. *Open daily, 1st Mar-30th Sept, 11am-5pm and Herts Schools Autumn Half Term week.* 01462 686775. (See Advert page 52.)

ⓒ
Schools
Open all year
🍃

Willers Mill Wildlife Park, Station Rd, **Shepreth,** is home to many species which have been donated or rescued including a wolf, tropical birds, Coati mundi, monkeys, guanacos, otters and pine martens as well as many domestic animals. Get closer to the animals in the petting field, where children can feed the goats, sheep, a donkey and deer. Feed the giant carp! There is an excellent adventure playground. Cafe facilities. Highly recommended. *Open daily, 10am-6pm in Summer, 10am-dusk in Winter.* 0891 715522. (See Advert page 50.)

ⓒ
Schools

Wimpole Home Farm, Royston, off the A603, is a 350 acre National Trust property within the grounds of Wimpole Hall and Park. There are lots of animals to see in the farmyard and there is a special children's corner with a picnic area, adventure playground and lambing weekends in March. *Open 8th Mar-2nd Nov, Tues-Thurs, Sat-Sun, Bank Hols. 10.30am-5pm. The Park is open all year daily.* 01223 207257. (See also "Discover" chapter.)

Ⓕ

Wood Green Animal Shelters, Godmanchester and Royston. See "Fun for Free" chapter.

C3
Ⓑ
Schools
Open all year
🍃

Capel Manor Gardens, Bullsmoor Lane, **Enfield,** (exit 25 off the M25/A10) 30 acres of superb gardens including wild areas and a maze to explore. See some rare breed farm animals and follow the garden trail. There is a garden gift shop and refreshments available. Ask about visits for groups. *Open daily, Mar-Oct, 10am-5.30pm, Nov-Feb, Mon-Fri, 10am-dusk.* 0181 366 4442.

Ⓑ
Schools
Open all year

Hayes Hill Farm & Holyfieldhall Farm, Waltham Abbey, part of the Lee Valley park, are off Stubbins Hall La, Crooked Mile. Traditional style farms with lots of animals to see at close quarters and a Friesian herd to watch being milked. *Open Mon-Fri, 10am-4.30pm; weekends and Bank Hol Mons, 10am-6pm.* 01992 892291.

Knebworth Park, includes a Deer Park with Red and Sika herd in the 250 acres of parkland. (See also "Discover", "Fun Parks" chapters and Advert page 44.)

C3
Ⓓ
Schools
Open all year
🍃

Paradise Wildlife Park, White Stubbs Lane, **Broxbourne.** Signed from Broxbourne and the A10, this is a marvellous interactive wildlife park. Many "hands on" animal experiences daily. New for 1997 is the Dr. Do & Dr. Littles Island Adventure Show, Pirates Cove play area, Mr. & Mrs. Noah's Indoor play area, Old MacDonalds Farm Yard and a big paddling pool. Other attractions include Woodland Railway, Adventure Playgrounds, Children's Rides, Woodland Walk. There is a full education and school visits programme available, phone for details. *Open daily 10am-6pm or dusk.* Information line 01992 468001. (See Advert page 52.)

Ⓑ
Schools
Open all year

RSPB Rye House Marsh Reserve, Rye Rd, **Hoddesdon.** This Nature Reserve is best approached from the A10 and is close to Rye House Railway. There is a wide variety of habitats on this riverside marsh and many different birds to see. *Open daily, 10am-dusk.* 01992 460031. Ⓕ to RSPB and YOC members.

Open all year
Ⓕ

RSPCA Animal Centre, Ridge. See "Fun for Free" chapter.

Ⓑ
Schools
Open all year

Water Hall Farm Craft Centre, Whitwell. Off the B651 Whitwell-Hitchin road. This farm has many farm animals in their natural environment. Wander through the paddocks and see rare breeds of cattle, sheep, pigs and poultry. You can feed and talk to the animals. Meet Bosun and Oscar, Tilley the Tamworth, Ronny and Katy and Gloria the Gloucester Old Spot. There are lots of rabbits and guinea pigs and in Spring or early Summer, new born lambs. Take a ride on the miniature railway. There are craft work shops and gift shop, plant centre and tearooms, a pine shop, wrought iron shop, delicatessen and a Bygone Barn. *Open Wed-Sun & Bank Hol Mons, 10am-5pm, 4pm in Winter, open daily in school hols.* 01438 871256. (See Advert page 54.)

NATURE

Map Ref: Please refer to map on page 4.
Price Codes for a family of four: Ⓐ: less than £5　Ⓑ: £5-£10　Ⓒ: £10-£15　Ⓓ: £15-£20　Ⓔ: £20-£30　Ⓖ:- Over £30　Ⓕ: Free
Schools: Range of educational opportunities available. 🍃 Birthday parties organised.

53

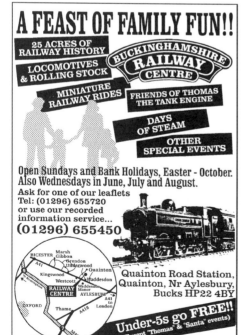

DISCOVER

Step back in time and find out about days gone by, or step into the future and imagine yourself in the next century. Art, history, science and technology find a place here.

Ⓑ **Claydon House,** Middle Claydon, **Buckingham,** is a perfect expression of Rococo decoration in England. The house has connections with the Civil War and a museum with mementoes of Florence Nightingale. *Open 22nd Mar-2nd Nov, Sat-Wed and Bank Hol Mon, 1-5pm. Last admissions 4.30 pm. Closed Good Fri.* 01296 730349.

Ⓑ **The Old Gaol Museum,** Market Hill, **Buckingham,** is housed in the Old
Schools Gaol, built in 1748. Visit the old cells and learn about Buckingham's past and the soldiers of the county. *Open Apr-Sept and Nov-Dec, Mon-Sat, 10am-4pm, some Thurs, Suns 2-4pm.* 01280 823020.

Ⓕ Schools **Buckinghamshire County Museum,** Church St., **Aylesbury.** See "Fun
Open all year for Free" chapter, Roald Dahl Children's Gallery below and Advert page 54.

Ⓒ **Buckinghamshire Railway Centre,** Quainton, 6 miles northwest of
Schools Aylesbury, is a working steam museum. Here visitors can experience the age of steam, riding in old style carriages behind full-sized steam locomotives and have fun travelling on the extensive miniature railway. Facilities include a gift and book shop, refreshment coach, picnic area and museum. Amongst the collection of over 35 locomotives, carriages and wagons are items from South Africa, the USA and Egypt, as well as the UK. "Thomas the Tank Engine" Days, 14th-15th Jun and 6th-7th Sept 1997. *Open Easter-end Oct, Suns and Bank Hol Mons; Weds in Jun, Jul and Aug, 11am-6pm. Open for viewing at other times.* 01296 655720 for free leaflet. (See Advert page 54.)

Ⓐ/Ⓑ **Hughenden Manor,** Hughenden, owned by the National Trust and set in
Schools large parkland on A4128, was the 19th century home of Benjamin Disraeli and now houses many mementoes. *Open 1st-30th Mar, Sat & Sun, 31st Mar-end Oct, Wed-Sun and Bank Hol Mons 1-5pm. Last admissions 4.30pm. Closed Good Fri. Park open all year.* 01494 532580.

Ⓐ/Ⓑ **Pitstone Green Farm Museum,** Pitstone, has a large collection of
Schools agricultural and rural bygones displayed against domestic, workshop backgrounds and listed farm buildings. Special activity open days with working stationary engines. *Museum open last Sun in month, May-Sept, 2.30-5pm. Activity days 2nd Sun Jun, Jul, Sept, 11am-5pm.* 01296 661997. Schools 01296 668083.

Ⓑ **The Roald Dahl Children's Gallery,** Buckinghamshire County
Schools Museum, Church Street, **Aylesbury.** Step into the magical world of Roald Dahl with
Open all year a visit to this new and exciting, hands-on museum. Have fun riding in the great
Ⓠ Glass Elevator, go inside the Giant Peach and discover Willy Wonka's inventions, let your imagination run wild! Schools have priority during term time. Under 3s are free and children under 8 must be accompanied by an adult. See entry in "Fun for Free" chapter for main museum. *Open, Tues-Sat, 10am-5pm, Sun & Bank Hols, 2-5pm. Last admission 4.15pm.* 01296 331441. (See Advert page 54.)

Ⓑ **West Wycombe Caves.** Explore these famous caves in the West Wycombe
Open all year Hill. See life sized models of the men connected with the Hell-Fire Club. West Wycombe Hill is ideal for picnics and walks. *Open daily, Mar-Oct, 11am-5.30pm, Nov-Feb, Sat, Sun and Bank Hols 11am-5.30pm.* 01494 533739.

Ⓕ Schools **Wycombe Local History and Chair Museum,** Castle Hill House,
Open all year Priory Avenue, **High Wycombe.** See "Fun for Free" chapter.

Map Ref: Please refer to map on page 4.
Price Codes for a family of four: Ⓐ: less than £5 Ⓑ: £5-£10 Ⓒ: £10-£15 Ⓓ: £15-£20 Ⓔ: £20-£30 Ⓖ:- Over £30 Ⓕ: Free
Schools: Range of educational opportunities available. Ⓠ Birthday parties organised.

A4 | ⓑ Schools | **The Blue Max Collection,** Wycombe Air Park, **Booker,** houses an historic collection of classic flying machines, many of which have appeared in films like "Indiana Jones", "Those Magnificent Men in their Flying Machines" and "Wind in the Willows". See the machines being restored as you walk around and visit the Souvenir shop. *Open Mar-Nov, Sat & Sun, 10am-5pm. Weekdays for parties only by prior arrangement.* 01494 529432.

B1 | ⓕ Schools Open all year | **Bedford Museum,** Castle Lane. See "Fun for Free" chapter.

ⓐ **Bromham Mill,** built in 17th century, is a restored historic watermill. Flour milling demonstrations on last Sun of month and Bank Hols during Summer. There is an associated display and an arts and crafts gallery. A pleasant riverside picnic site is close by. Guided tours and milling available for groups. *Open Mar-Oct, Wed-Sat, 12-4pm, Sun and Bank Hol Mons 10.30am-5pm.* 01234 824330.

ⓕ Schools Open all year **Cecil Higgins Art Gallery & Museum,** Castle Close, **Bedford.** See "Fun for Free" chapter.

ⓐ Schools **Elstow Moot Hall Museum.** The Moot Hall is managed as a museum containing a permanent exhibition relating to life in the village of Elstow in the 17th century. *Open Apr-Oct, Tues-Thurs, Sat-Sun and Bank Hols 2-5pm.* 01234 266889.

ⓕ **Stevington Postmill.** See "Fun for Free" chapter.

B2 | © Schools Open all year | **Bletchley Park,** Bletchley, **Milton Keynes,** was home to the allied security services during World War II. Visit the numerous displays reflecting aspects of the life during the war and see "Colossus", the computer which helped break Hitler's messages to his Generals. *Open every other weekend commencing 11/12th Jan, 10.30am-5pm. Last admission, 3.30pm.* 01908 640404.

ⓑ Schools Open all year **Stondon Transport Museum,** Station Rd., **Lower Stondon.** Probably the largest private collection of vehicles in Europe. Examples of all modes of transport from early cars and motor bikes to present day models. Full size replica of HMS 'Endeavour' to be completed in 1997, showing conditions on ships in earlier times. Picnic area. *Open daily, 10am-5pm.* 01462 850339.

© / ⓓ Schools Open all year **Woburn Abbey** on the A4012, close to M1, Jn 13, has been home to the Dukes of Bedford for over 350 years and houses private collections of famous paintings, as well as porcelain, furniture and silver. The Abbey is set in 3,000 acres of beautiful parkland in which nine species of deer can be seen. *Open Sat/Sun only to 22nd Mar then daily 23rd Mar-2nd Nov, 11am-4pm, Suns, 11am-5pm.* 01525 290666. Children under 12 free Abbey admission. (See 'Nature' and 'Fun Parks' for Woburn Safari Park and Advert page 46.)

B3 | ⓕ | **Berkhamsted Castle.** See "Fun for Free" chapter.

© Schools 🎈 **Chiltern Open Air Museum,** Newland Park, Gorelands Lane, **Chalfont St. Giles.** Well-signed from neighbouring main roads this is an unusual museum spread over a large area, containing over twenty rescued old buildings and showing their development through the ages, many with displays of farm tools and equipment. Visit the Iron Age house and a blacksmith's forge, in use on special event days which include Children's Days (24th-25th Aug). Farm animals bring the Victorian farmyard alive and there are regular craft demonstrations. There is a pleasant woodland walk and tours around the exhibits are available for booked parties. The museum is also suited to school age children. School parties are very welcome by prior arrangement and activity guides are available. Information Line 01494 872163. *Open 25th Mar-2nd Nov Tues-Fri, 2-6pm, Sat, Sun, Bank Hols and throughout Aug 11am-6pm. Closed Mons all season.* (See Advert page 54.)

ⓕ Schools **The John Dony Field Centre,** Luton. See "Fun for Free" chapter.

Map Ref: Please refer to map on page 4.
Price Codes for a family of four: Ⓐ: less than £5 Ⓑ: £5-£10 Ⓒ: £10-£15 Ⓓ: £15-£20 Ⓔ: £20-£30 Ⓖ: Over £30 Ⓕ: Free
Schools: Range of educational opportunities available. 🎈 Birthday parties organised.

56

B3

⒜ Schools
Open all year
Kingsbury Watermill, St. Michaels Street, **St. Albans,** spans the River Ver. See the working waterwheel, farm implements and the "Hertfordshire Pudding Stone". *Open Tues-Sat, 11am-6pm, Sun, 12-6pm; Winter closing, 5pm.* 01727 853502.

⒡ Schools
Open all year
Luton Museum and Art Gallery, Wardown Park. See "Fun for Free" chapter.

⒝
Schools
Mosquito Aircraft Museum, Salisbury Hall, **St. Albans.** The original plans to develop the Mosquito were drawn up on this historic site. Many other aircraft exhibits and you can see restoration work in progress. There are regular flying displays and a shop for visitors. *Open Mar-Oct, Tues, Thurs and Sat. 2-5.30pm, Sun and Bank Hols 10-30am-5.30pm.* 01727 822051.

⒡
The Mossman Collection, Luton. See "Fun for Free" chapter.

⒡ Schools
Museum of St. Albans, Hatfield Road. See "Fun for Free" chapter.

⒜
Schools
🎈
Redbournbury Mill, signed off Redbourn Road, **St. Albans.** This recently restored watermill was once owned by the Abbey of St. Albans and has an unusual mill-working layout. Special displays and open days arranged with local groups and societies. *Open Mar-Oct, Sun. 2.30-5.30pm.* ⒡ *Bank Hols Sun/Mons and events throughout the year 10.30am-5.30pm* (charge payable). 01582 792874.

Schools
Open all year
St. Albans Cathedral, Sumpter Yard. This award-winning Education Centre offers a wide range of Cathedral trails and practical workshops to tie in with the National Curriculum demands for schools. From maths to history, and religious studies to technology, the possibilities are endless. Phone the Education Officer on 01727 836223 for "A Guide for Teachers" which gives information on how to book.

⒝
Open all year
St. Albans Organ Museum, 320 Camp Road. This museum houses dance band organs, two theatre organs (a Rutt and a Wurlitzer), also pianos and musical boxes amongst its exhibits. Recitals every Sunday. Might be noisy for very young children. *Open Sun, 2.15-4.30pm.* 01727 851557.

⒡ Schools
Open all year
Stockwood Craft Museum and Gardens, Farley Hill, **Luton.** See "Fun for Free" chapter.

⒝
Schools
Open all year
Verulamium Museum, St. Michaels, **St. Albans,** is an award-winning museum depicting everyday life in Roman Britain. A short walk from the museum brings you to the hypocaust, city wall and Roman theatre. There is a car park adjacent. *Open Mon-Sat, 10am-5pm; Sun, 2-5pm.* 01727 819339.

⒝
Schools
Open all year
The Walter Rothschild Zoological Museum, Akeman Street, Tring. There are thousands of animals, birds and fish perfectly preserved in this branch of the Natural History Museum. Look out for the polar bear and giant tortoise. *Open Mon-Sat, 10am-5pm, Sun, 2-5pm.* 01442 824181.

⒡ Schools
Open all year
Watford Museum, 194 Lower High Street. See "Fun for Free" chapter.

 B4

⒝
Schools
🎈
Bekonscot Model Village, Warwick Road, **Beaconsfield.** Well signed from all directions and trapped in time, this pre-war model village covers over one and a half acres and is one of the finest of its kind. Created in 1929, it includes miniature street scenes, factories, castles, churches and shops. It is planted with over 800 conifers. A superb model railway weaves its way around the village and there are up to six trains running at any one time. With a fairground, village green, harbour and a coal mine to see, Bekonscot is well worth a visit and is popular with adults and children alike. There are also two picnic areas and a children's playground. *Open 15th Feb-2nd Nov, daily, 10am-5pm.* 01494 672919. (See Advert page 58.)

DISCOVER

Map Ref: Please refer to map on page 4.
Price Codes for a family of four: ⒜: less than £5 ⒝: £5-£10 ⒞: £10-£15 ⒟: £15-£20 ⒠: £20-£30 ⒢: Over £30 ⒡: Free
Schools: Range of educational opportunities available. 🎈 Birthday parties organised.

ⓐ Schools
Open all year

Ashwell Village Museum, Swan Street, reflects the life of a typical English village with a wide range of relics including children's toys, dolls and prams. Favourite exhibits include a mummified black rat and a man trap. *Open Sun & Bank Hol Mons, 2.30-5pm.* 01462 742956.

ⓓ
Schools
Open all year

Duxford Airfield, a few miles east of Royston on A505. (use Jn 10 off M11). See many famous aircraft in the huge hangers and visit an early Concorde on the runway. A new Land Warfare Hall depicts battle scenes and in a simulator you can fly in a dogfight. *Open daily, 10am-6pm, 4pm in Winter.* 01223 835000.

ⓕ Schools
Open all year

First Garden City Heritage Museum, Letchworth. See "Fun for Free" chapter.

ⓕ Schools
Open all year

Letchworth Museum, The Broadway. See "Fun for Free" chapter.

ⓐ

Royston Cave. Discovered in 1742, this unique underground cave lies at the end of a passage off Melbourn Street in the centre of town. The cave has mediaeval wall carvings. The entrance is beneath a shop. *Open Easter-Sept, Sat, Sun, Bank Hol Mons, 2.30-5pm.* 01763 245484.

ⓓ / ⓔ
Schools
Open all year

The Shuttleworth Collection, Old Warden Aerodrome, **Biggleswade,** has over 30 aircraft covering 70 years of aviation and all exhibits are airworthy and fly regularly. There is also a display of motor vehicles, carriages and vintage bicycles. Flying displays are held on the first Sunday of each month. *Open daily, 10am-5pm, (4pm in Winter). Closed Christmas and New Year.* 01767 627288.

ⓒ

Wimpole Hall, north of **Royston,** on the Herts/Cambs border, off A603. A spectacular 18th Century mansion, owned by the National Trust. Children's guide available. The adjacent Home Farm is worth a visit. *Open 22nd Mar-2nd Nov, Tues-Thurs, Sat-Sun, 1-5pm, all Bank Hol Sun/Mons 11am-5pm.* (See "Nature" chapter.)

C3

Ⓐ Schools **Cromer Windmill,** Cromer, Nr. **Stevenage**. The only surviving postmill in Hertfordshire, still undergoing restoration. *Open May-Sept. 2nd & 4th Sats, Sun and Bank Hols. 2.30-5pm.* 01438 861662.

Ⓐ Schools Open all year **The Forge Museum and Victorian Cottage Garden,** High Street, Much Hadham. This living museum was the village forge from 1811 to 1983. The Victorian cottage garden contains a rare bee shelter. *Open Sat, 10.30am-4pm, Sun, 12-4pm. Phone 01763 843759 for groups and visits by arrangement.* 01279 843301.

Ⓓ Schools **Hatfield House,** on the A1000, opposite rail station, Junction 4 A1(M). A delightful and educational day out for all age groups. Hatfield is a superb Jacobean House dating from 1611 with a fine collection of pictures, furniture, tapestries and armoury. In the beautiful gardens stands the Old Palace, childhood home of Elizabeth I. The Great Park provides nature trails, an adventure play area, the National collection of over 3,000 Model Soldiers and a William IV kitchen. Guided tours run at regular intervals, ensuring that the content is tailored to age group, interest and language. *Open end Mar-mid Oct; House 12-4pm; Park 10.30am-8pm, Sun 1.30-4.30pm. Closed Mons and Good Fri. (No guided tours on Sun.)* 01707 262823. (See Advert page 58.)

Ⓕ **Hertford Castle.** See "Fun for Free" chapter.

Ⓕ Schools Open all year **Hertford Museum,** Bull Plain. See "Fun for Free" chapter.

Ⓕ Schools Open all year **Hitchin Museum and Art Gallery,** Paynes Park. See "Fun for Free" chapter.

Ⓒ Schools **Knebworth House.** Magnificent stately home of the Lytton family since 1490. A spectacular palace with high Gothic decoration. Formal gardens which include the re-instated Knebworth Maze. *Open as for Knebworth Park (See "Fun Parks" chapter) except House open 12 noon-5pm. Closed Mons but open Bank Hol Mons.* 01438 812661. (See Advert page 44.)

C3

Ⓕ Open all year **Lee Valley Park Countryside Centre,** Waltham Abbey. See "Fun for Free" chapter.

Ⓕ Schools **Lowewood Museum,** High Street, Hoddesdon. See "Fun for Free" chapter.

Ⓕ Schools **Mill Green Mill,** Mill Green, Hatfield. See "Fun for Free" chapter.

Ⓕ Schools **Mill Green Museum,** Mill Green, Hatfield. See "Fun for Free" chapter.

Ⓐ Schools Open all year **Rhodes Memorial Museum,** South Road, Bishops Stortford, is the birthplace of Cecil Rhodes, empire builder, statesman and financier. His life and times are depicted here, together with some general exhibits of local history. *Open Tues-Sat, 10am-4pm.* 01279 651746.

Ⓐ **Rye House,** Hoddesdon, houses a small exhibition revealing its history. *Open Easter-Sept, Sat 1-5pm; Sun & Bank Hol Mons, 11am-5pm. Weekdays in Summer school hols, 11am-5pm.* 01992 713838.

Ⓐ Schools **Scott's Grotto,** Scotts Road, Ware. Remarkable underground passages and chambers extend 67' into the hillside and are patterned with shells, flints and pebbles. Don't forget your torches! *Open 1st Apr-30th Sept, Sat and Bank Hol Mons, 2-4.30pm.* 01920 464131.

Ⓐ Schools Open all year **Welwyn Roman Baths,** under A1(M) at A1000 exit, off Welwyn by-pass roundabout. An ingeniously preserved site showing the layout and workings of a Roman bathing suite, now installed in a vault under the A1(M). Clearly visible exhibits and a fascinating insight into this important part of Roman life. Children Ⓕ. Adults small charge. *Open Thurs, Fri, Sat, Sun and Bank Hols. 2-5pm (or dusk).* (Mill Green Museum for details). 01707 271362. (See Advert page 12.)

DISCOVER

Map Ref: Please refer to map on page 4.
Price Codes for a family of four: Ⓐ: less than £5 Ⓑ: £5-£10 Ⓒ: £10-£15 Ⓓ: £15-£20 Ⓔ: £20-£30 Ⓖ:- Over £30 Ⓕ: Free
Schools: Range of educational opportunities available. ● Birthday parties organised.

MAP

Try these puzzles. There are lots of clues on the pages but all the answers can be found on the key of an Ordnance Survey Landranger map.

JOIN WITH A LINE

Picnic area

Windmill

Telephone

Golf Course

Wood

Church with spire

Campsite

LET'S GO FOR A WALK ...

This family started at the i and armed with ideas, set off for the day. They chose a which went across a and up a hill. They came to a P at a lovely . There was a , so they stopped and fortunately for everyone there was also a **PC**. Later on they set off down the hill on a and in the valley they crossed a over the river. Ahead was a village and they could just see a beyond the . Mother posted a card at the **P** and father looked out for the **PH**, but it was closed. Everyone was a little tired now, so they went to the local to wait for the train home.

PUZZLES
ANAGRAM TRAIL

© Crown copyright 1997

KEY:
Telephone, **PH** Public House, **P** Post Office,
Church with tower, ▪▪▪▪▪ Footpath,
Bridleway.

Solve the anagrams and find me - if you can! (Grid Ref is not jumbled!)

I FELT YM MEOH TA KARP MARF RIGD FER: 977 874 DAN KAWDEL HORNT STEW LOANG HET DOAR OT SRADGON. I DERTUN FELT STAP HET RCCHHU DAN STAP RAMON MARF OT HET RACORCSDOS. I DERTUN GIRTH DAN HENT GIRTH GANIA TONO A POOFHATT. XTEN FELT NO HET POOFHATT HENT TRONH OT THOCRALN. TA HET DOAR, I DERTUN FELT STAP HET BUP HENT I POPSTED OT ESE YM NERFID TA YERRP REGEN.
Did I go by the shortest route ?

DE-CODE TO HELP FIND YOUR WAY!

My 1st is in **ROCK** and also in **CLIFF**   (   )
My 2nd is in **PLOT** and also in **COURSE**   (   )
My 3rd is in **CAMP** but not in **PACK**   (   )
My 4th is in **PATH** but not in **TRACK**   (   )
My 5th is in **EAST** but not in **WEST**   (   )
My 6th is in **COAST** but not in **BEACH**   (   )
My 7th is in **SOUTH** but not in **NORTH**   (   )

FAMILY PUBS

Times are changing and so are the pubs. A selection here of the best we have found which welcome families and provide some facilities, either outdoor or indoor, to entertain children.

Hanslope, The Globe Inn, Hartwell Rd., 01908 510336. On the Northampton border in the Long Street area, this cosy pub has a variety of play equipment. The restaurant welcomes families.

Aylesbury, The Crooked Billet is on the A41 at Ham Green, Nr. Kingswood, 01296 770239 and has a garden with swings, slide and climbing frame.

Bledlow, The Lions at Bledlow, 01844 343345. Set in the heart of the Chilterns, this large, traditional pub has a dining room where children are welcome. Plenty of seating outside on the green. There is a ghost, but don't worry, it's friendly.

Carlton, Royal Oak, Bridgend, 01234 720441, has an extensive games/family room, with toys, a piano, various coin machines and board games. Lots of comfortable seating. Outside in the garden is a variety of play equipment and ride-on toys as well as a number of small animals.

Keysoe, The Chequers, Kimbolton Rd., 01234 708678. Free House with an extensive function room open for family use. Large, neat garden with a Wendy house and slide, Globe, Herbie Tree and swings. *Closed on Tuesdays.*

Hexton, The Raven, off B655, 01582 881209. Pleasant, busy village pub with a pretty, fenced garden full of play equipment, including swings, roundabout, climbing frame, slide and Wendy house. Children's menu available.

Milton Keynes, The Wayfarer, Brickhill St., Willen Lake. 01908 675222, is in a lovely position overlooking the lake. There is an enclosed terrace with tables and chairs from where you can watch the watersports in action.

Southill, White Horse, High St. 01462 813364. A pub with a difference. Around the large garden runs a miniature railway in the Summer. There is a variety of play equipment with swings, slides and a see-saw. If the weather is inclement children are welcome in the restaurant.

Abbots Langley, The Royal Oak, Kitters Green. 01923 265163. Enclosed garden with a wooden fort, horseshoe pitch, toddlers area with toys, swings, see-saw and slide. Children can be watched through patio doors.

Bricket Wood, Moor Mill, Smug Oak Lane, 01727 875557. This converted 18th century water-mill has a well-appointed family room with comfortable seating. Outside wildlife wander around the grounds and there is a variety of play equipment.

Houghton Regis, The Chequers Family Inn, East End North, 01582 865970, offers an impressive range of facilities for families including an enclosed garden, children's play areas both outside and indoors, family room. Holiday activities and children's menu.

Kensworth, The Horse & Jockey, Watling St., 01582 840509. Attached to a Travel Inn on the A5 south of Dunstable, this pub/restaurant has super indoor facilities, including adventure play area with ball pool, scramble rides and games machines. Separate toddler play room with video. Indoor family area and outdoor play area well fenced with tables around it.

Kings Langley, Langleys, Hempstead Rd., 01923 263150. This large, imposing pub-restaurant has a 'Funky Forest' indoor play area for under 5s with a ball pond and climbing equipment. Outside is a well-equipped playground with a multitude of multiplay equipment.

Luton, The Barn Owl, Farley Hill, 01582 29532. This family pub has a large assortment of play equipment, including a climbing frame, rope mast, swings and slide. Inside there is comfortable seating, games, jigsaws, games machine and indoor adventure playground.

Map Ref: Please refer to map on page 4.
Price Codes for a family of four: Ⓐ: less than £5 Ⓑ: £5-£10 Ⓒ: £10-£15 Ⓓ: £15-20 Ⓔ: £20-£30 Ⓖ:- Over £30 Ⓕ: Free
Schools: Range of educational opportunities available. ♠ Birthday parties organised.

62

B3 **Wheathampstead**, Wicked Lady, Nomansland, 01582 832128. The grounds of this large pub feature a play bus on a grassed area surrounded by well-maintained play equipment. During school holidays there are puppet and magic shows as well as face painting. Inside there is a pleasant family conservatory.

C3 **Hoddesdon**, Fish and Eels, Dobbs Weir Rd., 01992 715757. On the Herts/Essex border, this popular pub on the River Lee has a children's room with video, a climbing frame and Lego. Outside is a large patio area adjacent to the river, plus an activity area with swings and a climbing frame.

Hooks Cross, The Three Horseshoes, on A602 nr. Stevenage, 01920 830391. This pub has a very large garden with a seemingly endless variety of swings, slides and climbing equipment as well as a duck pond, aviary and an area with tame rabbits. Organised children's events occasionally. Children's menu.

Knebworth, The Station, Park Lane, 01438 812224. Conservatory has TV, a video game, a large blackboard, Lego and comfortable seating. In the garden there is a slide, climbing apparatus and tables. Good stop for Knebworth Park. *Open all day.*

Stevenage, The Pear Tree, Valley Way, 01438 351715. Lying in the Shephall area, this pub has a family conservatory and gardens. There is a fenced-in play area with see-saw and other multi-play equipment, all on a bark surface. Inside the conservatory are toys, a TV and video games machine. *Open all day.*

Welwyn Garden City, Ludwick Arms, Hall Grove, 01707 323623. Not only a well-kept play area outside on a bark surface with rocking animals, slides and swings but also a super family conservatory with drawing pads with space on the wall to display your work, a high chair and a TV showing cartoons and films.

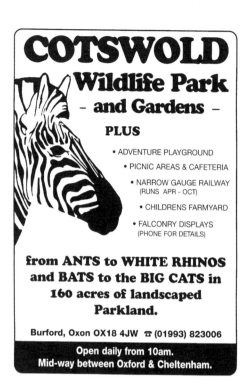

BEYOND

BERKSHIRE

© Schools 🔍 **Coral Reef,** Coral Reef, Nine Mile Ride, is a warm, tranquil, tropical paradise to relax in or a wildly exciting water wonderland to have a lot of fun in. There are fast, converging rapids, giant flumes and erupting geysers for those with daring and a pirate ship for those with an adventurous spirit. Younger children will be more than happy in the gentle Corals Pools or under the Emerald Forest Rain Cloud. There is a White Volcano, a Lazy River, Bubble Lounger, Sauna World (adults only) and a health suite to enjoy; something for everyone and there are poolside sun beds, cafes, bars and restaurant areas to enjoy as well. Birthday parties are well catered for. Under 8s must be accompanied by an adult (Maximum of 2 under 8s per adult). Full programme operates from 9am each weekend and daily from 10.30am during school holidays. During term time an off peak programme operates. Phone for other times. 24 hour information service on 01344 862484. (See Advert inside front cover.)

© Schools 🔍 **LEGOLAND**® Windsor, in a beautiful setting of wooded parkland, is full of surprises and will delight and involve the whole family. The approach drive sets the scene and from the beginning you can see the Park spread beneath you as part of a panoramic view. Walk the steep slope or take the hill train to the heart of the Park from where you can explore a variety of different themed areas. Opportunities await round every corner to awaken the creativity of children of all ages and to fire every imagination. Pan for gold, splash on the Pirate Falls flume ride, get lost in the mazes, walk the nature trail, brave the Spinning Spider or watch one of the five shows. Children can earn a Driving Licence, drive a power boat, take a helicopter ride, explore the Wild Woods and much more. Miniland recreates scenes around Europe in astonishing detail from 20 million LEGO® bricks! Don't miss the brilliant Imagination Centre, the "intelligent" pedal powered monocycle ride and the new space tower ride, on which children can pull themselves up to the top of the tower by rope, to examine the hovering space ship, then "abseil" to the bottom. Park capacity will be controlled to ensure maximum enjoyment for visitors, so an advance booking system operates. Book in advance or just turn up at the gate. Good food, birthday packages, season tickets and an educational service are all on offer. 0990 04 04 04 for bookings hotline. (See Advert inside back cover.)

ESSEX

© Schools Open all year **Mole Hall Wildlife Park,** Widdington, just south of Newport, near Saffron Walden, covers some 20 acres and has lovely woodland and waterside paths. A wide variety of animals include great favourites like otters, chimps and Vietnamese pot-bellied pigs. See the mystical Kenyan Eagle Owls, the leopard-like Serval Cat and Formosan Sika Deer, which are extinct in the wild. A great attraction during the Summer is the Butterfly Pavilion housing a beautiful collection of these colourful creatures in jungle-like surroundings. School parties are particularly well catered for here and work sheets and teachers' packs are available. *Open daily, 10.30am-6pm (or dusk). Butterfly House open Easter-end Oct.* 01799 540400. (See Advert page 63.)

NORTHAMPTONSHIRE

Ⓑ Schools Open all year **The Canal Museum,** Stoke Bruerne. Housed in a restored cornmill, situated adjacent to the Grand Union Canal, the museum vividly portrays the heritage of 200 years of inland waterways. A fascinating and colourful insight can be gained on every aspect of the waterways as you explore the three floors of exhibits. There are working models, videos, pictorial and three dimensional displays and a full size replica of a boat cabin traditionally decorated and furnished. Outside watch the boats passing through the locks or take a pleasant stroll to the Blisworth Tunnel. Alternatively take a gentle cruise along the canal on one of the trip boats operating from Stoke Bruerne. Extensive school party facilities include a comprehensive education pack. *Open Easter-Oct, daily, 10am-6pm, Oct-Easter, closes 4pm and all day Mon, Nov-Mar.* 01604 862229. (See Advert page 64.)

BEYOND

Price Codes for a family of four: Ⓐ: less than £5 Ⓑ: £5-£10 Ⓒ: £10-£15 Ⓓ: £15-£20 Ⓔ: £25-£30 Ⓖ:- Over £30 Ⓕ: Free
Schools: Range of educational opportunities available. 🔍 Birthday parties organised.

65

(A)
Schools
Q

Wicksteed Park, Kettering, signposted from junction 10 of the A14, is the oldest leisure park of its type in the country. The 148 acres of parkland and lake has over 40 attractions including two roller coasters, a double pirate ship, dodgems, Cine 2000 and a 10 minute train ride. Get soaked on the water chute and the nautic jets, pretend to be Damon Hill on the racing car circuit, experience 'G' force on the rotor ride, feel disorientated on the gyroscopes or enjoy a leisurely row on the lake. There is plenty for younger children with their own favourite rides, and an excellent free playground area. How many slides can you count? There are food outlets and seated catering for 600. Pay as you go vouchers or unlimited rides wristbands can be purchased. Please ring for prices. *Open daily, 22nd Mar-2nd Nov from 10am. Closing times vary according to time of year and weather; please phone to check.* 01536 512475. (See Advert page 64.)

OXFORDSHIRE

(D)
Schools
Open all year
Q

Cotswold Wildlife Park, Burford, occupies 160 acres of gardens and parkland with a wide variety of animals to be seen as you walk around. The wildlife varies from reptiles to tarantulas, penguins to rhinos as well as endangered Asiatic lions, Amur leopards and Red Pandas, in large enclosures. Extensive picnic lawns, shaded by oaks and California Redwoods, also provide a setting for a large adventure playground and children's farmyard. A brass-rubbing centre and cafeteria are located in the listed Victorian Manor in the centre of the Park. During the Summer there are special events and a narrow-gauge railway runs from April to October. The Park encourages school parties and has all-round pushchair and wheelchair access. *Open daily at 10am. Last admissions 5pm, Summer, 4pm, Winter.* 01993 823006. (See Advert page 64.)

(B)
Schools
Open all year
Q

The Water Fowl Sanctuary and Children's Farm, Wigginton Heath, off the A361 Banbury to Chipping Norton road, is a wonderful place to take children, whatever the weather. Mix with the rabbits and feed the many birds and animals with grain on sale, or bring your own. There is a trail laid out to follow around the two thousand birds and animals on view. Throughout the year there are many baby animals and birds for you to pick up, cuddle and want to take home! Easy to read and interesting information tells you about many of the birds and animals including goats, sheep, ponies, cattle, pigs, ducks, swans, ostriches, emus and rheas from a bygone age. There is an adventure playground to enjoy. Covered picnic areas are available. Practical clothing and footwear, especially wellies, if wet, are recommended for a visit to this Conservation Award haven. School parties are very welcome with quizzes, National Curriculum worksheets and free promotional video available. Incubators may be loaned by schools. *Open daily, except Christmas Day, 10.30am-6pm, or dusk.* 01608 730252. Free parking, free pre-visit for teachers, 10 people 10% discount if pre-booked. (See Advert page 64.)

SURREY

(G)
Schools

The Great Thorpe Park, Staines Rd., Chertsey, located on the A320 between Staines and Chertsey, with easy access from jns. 11 & 13 off M25, is a marvellous family leisure park spread over an attractive 500 acre site with a wide variety of excellent attractions on offer. There are rides to suit all ages from the refreshing tea cup ride, the Flying Fish rollercoaster, the wet and wild Loggers Leap, Depth Charge and Thunder River rides to the one and only of its kind: X:/No Way Out. This is the only backwards plummeting ride, in total darkness, in the world, and promises to be like nothing else you have ever experienced or imagined! Enter if you dare, there is no way out! To slow the adrenalin rate, take a boat or train to the Great Thorpe Farm, where you can step back in time with the animals, relax on the Fantasy Reef beach, or wander around Ranger Country for some jungle adventures and a swing on Mr Monkey's Banana Ride. Excellent value for money, there are many schemes for purchasing tickets by phone in advance, cost reductions on "Plan-Ahead" tickets and a new Parent and Toddler Pass which is a must to look out for in 1997. With so much to see and do, it is hard to fit everything into just one day - you may have to go again and again! Excellent educational material for school parties. *Open daily, Mar-Oct.* For full opening details, phone the Information Hotline: 01932 562633. (See Advert pages 1 & 2.)

Price Codes for a family of four: **(A)**: less than £5 **(B)**: £5-£10 **(C)**: £10-£15 **(D)**: £15-£20 **(E)**: £25-£30 **(G)**:- Over £30 **(F)**: Free
Schools: Range of educational opportunities available. Q Birthday parties organised.

Let's Go to France

Folkestone to Calais...

...in around 35 minutes

It is convenient and easy whatever the weather. Just turn up with your car at the Folkestone terminal, junction 11a, off the M20 motorway and travel when you want to. Services are fast and frequent in peak periods. You don't have to book. Simply buy a ticket on arrival at the terminal or get an open ticket in advance. For more information call 0990 353535.

le Shuttle

100 MISSIONS A DAY

ABCDRBQCALAISTRLONBFENGLANDHRFVBF

Try this word search on the way.

Find:
Folkestone,
Calais,
England,
France.

MBVFTFOLKESTONERNVKDLSLFRANCEMCTEDKM

5

Return Trips on Le Shuttle TO BE WON

(Valid for one car with passengers)

ll you have to
o is answer
ne following
uestion:

hich motorway
ads to the
olkestone
erminal?

| M25 | M2 | M20 |

Send you answer, name and address on a postcard to:
Le Shuttle Competition c/o Cube Publications Bank House, Mavins Road, Farnham, Surrey GU9 8JS

Make sure your entries reach us by 30th November 1997. The winners will be the first correct entries drawn. Winners will be notified by post during December 1997. No responsibility can be accepted for entries lost, defaced or delayed in the post. No correspondence can be entered into and the decision of the publishing company is final.

LET'S GO with the CHILDREN guides available in other areas at a special discounted price, only from the publishers, using the voucher stamps below.

Beds, Bucks, Herts (BBH)
Berks, Bucks, Oxon (BBO)
Cotswolds, Bath & Bristol (CBB)
Essex & Suffolk, inc Cambridge (EXS)
Hants & Dorset inc Salisbury (HAD)

Kent (KNT)
Middle England
(Leics, Northants, Rutland, Warks) (MEN)
Surrey (SRY)
Sussex (SSX)

Normal retail price is £2.25 for MEN edition, £2.65 for all others.
Normal mail order price is £2.70 or £3.20 per edition inc p&p. Send in the relevant voucher stamp with the reply slip and pay just £2.20 per edition inc p&p.

£1 OFF Mail order price of BBH EDITION OF **Let's Go with the Children 1997**
Valid only using reply slip below, and direct from the publishers. Valid until 30th December 1997 and only while stocks last.

£1 OFF Mail order price of BBO EDITION OF **Let's Go with the Children 1997**
Valid only using reply slip below, and direct from the publishers. Valid until 30th December 1997 and only while stocks last.

£1 OFF Mail order price of CBB EDITION OF **Let's Go with the Children 19**
Valid only using reply slip below, and direct fr the publishers. Valid until 30th December 19 and only while stocks last.

£1 OFF Mail order price of EXS EDITION OF **Let's Go with the Children 1997**
Valid only using reply slip below, and direct from the publishers. Valid until 30th December 1997 and only while stocks last.

£1 OFF Mail order price of HAD EDITION OF **Let's Go with the Children 1997**
Valid only using reply slip below, and direct from the publishers. Valid until 30th December 1997 and only while stocks last.

£1 OFF Mail order price of KNT EDITION OF **Let's Go with the Children 19**
Valid only using reply slip below, and direct fr the publishers. Valid until 30th December 19 and only while stocks last.

50P OFF Mail order price of MEN EDITION OF **Let's Go with the Children 1997**
Valid only using reply slip below, and direct from the publishers. Valid until 30th December 1997 and only while stocks last.

£1 OFF Mail Order price of SRY EDITION OF **Let's Go with the Children 1997**
Valid only using reply slip below, and direct from the publishers. Valid until 30th December 1997 and only while stocks last.

£1 OFF Mail Order price of SSX EDITION OF **Let's Go with the Children 1**
Valid only using reply slip below, and direct f the publishers. Valid until 30th December 19 and only while stocks last.

I enclose Vouchers towards the cost of one copy each of:

☐ BBH ☐ BBO ☐ CBB ☐ EXS ☐ HAD ☐ KNT ☐ MEN ☐ SRY ☐ SSX (PLEASE TIC

I enclose a cheque for £.................made payable to Cube Publications
(£2.20 per copy including p&p if order is accompanied by appropriate voucher stamp).

Name..
Address..
....
Town...Postcode...

Please send enclosures to "Let's Go Counties Offer",
Cube Publications, Bank House, Mavins Road, Farnham, Surrey GU9 8JS